Kleptomania

Kleptomania

The Compulsion to Steal – What Can Be Done?

by Marcus J. Goldman, M.D.

New Horizon Press

Far Hills, New Jersey

Requests for permission should be addressed to:

New Horizon Press

P.O. Box 669

Far Hills, New Jersey 07931

Goldman, Marcus J.

Kleptomania: The Compulsion to Steal—What Can Be Done?

Library of Congress Catalog Card Number: 97-066565

ISBN: 0-88282-158-X

Interior Design: Howard Simpson

New Horizon Press

Manufactured in the U.S.A.

2001   2000   1999   1998 /   5   4   3   2   1

This book is dedicated to Dr. Louis Ripich and Mrs. Hillins, whose collective wisdom, guidance, and humility made a difference.

Contents

Prologue

The ideas for *Kleptomania,* the results of which I published in *The American Journal of Psychiatry* in 1991, developed from data I gathered as a resident and clinical fellow in psychiatry at Harvard Medical School. When I began studying at Harvard, my training was narrowly focused on the diagnosis and treatment of the most severely mentally ill, which, due to their dramatic nature, like hallucinations and delusions, were often easy to detect. Nonetheless, I had always been interested in emotional disorders with symptoms far less obvious, and eventually became fascinated by patients' attempts to calm themselves in non-traditional ways. Unlike those who were grossly disturbed, these people rarely, if ever, came forward for treatment—either tending or needing to keep their symptoms secret.

Kleptomania is one such "secretive disorder," characterized by the impulsive theft of unneeded objects which are often easily afforded by the person taking them. The *DSM-IV,* a handbook of psychiatric diagnoses, lists five so-called

"Disorders of Impulse Control:" intermittent explosive disorder (sudden aggressive and often violent behavior), trichotillomania (pulling out one's own hair), pathological gambling, pyromania (fire setting) and kleptomania. Of the five, kleptomania appears to be unique. It seems the least obviously dramatic or attention-seeking, and least destructive. It's basic secrecy makes it perhaps the most difficult impulse disorder to detect. These facts place those suffering from kleptomania among the loneliest and most isolated of patients suffering from impulse disorders.

THE COMPLEXITY OF STEALING: NOT MERELY A MATTER OF THEFT

I soon became aware that people suffering from kleptomania also suffered from a variety of other intense emotional conflicts. In fact, stealing represented only a part of what appeared to be an entire set of specific behaviors. I found that patients I treated felt baffled by their symptoms and, often, had intensely conflicted feelings about themselves. Their dismay was intensified by their own apparent unwillingness to share their concerns with mental health professionals.

While the causes of kleptomania remain unclear, there are remarkable person-to-person patient similarities. Some common signs exist:

Depression and Despair. Depression, an emotion common to all human beings at one time or another, is characterized by feelings of sadness, irritability, fatigue, diminished energy levels, and lack of pleasure. An emotion that can disrupt sleep and appetite, it can, in its most severe form, result in suicide. In its mildest form, sufferers can carry on their lives in an almost ordinary manner. In a severe form, it can leave them disabled. People suffering from kleptomania appear to experience significant levels of episodic or permanent sadness. A relationship may also exist (although the extent is not clear) between eating disorders (which are often associated with depression) and kleptomania.

Anxiety. Encountered by almost everyone to some degree, anxiety can become severe. Fearful, tense, and nervous, sufferers in a severe form exist in a perpetual state of "readiness," and can honestly expect "the worst." Like depression, anxiety can also effect sleep and appetite. In one form or another, we have all experienced anxiety when faced with a frightening experience, such as taking an important test or finding ourselves in a dangerous situation. In its extreme forms, however, anxiety, also like depression, can be crippling. Kleptomania sufferers experience inordinate amounts of anxiety.

Isolation. Because relationships can be difficult to maintain, people suffering from kleptomania may feel lonely and isolated. They may feel poorly understood and unsupported.

Mood Swings. Sufferers may often find themselves plagued by chronic irritability, anger, or the inability to control rapid mood swings. The origin and meanings of such mood changes are poorly understood by sufferers and may lead to confusion about their identities.

Secrets. Secrecy seems to be central to kleptomania. While harboring secrets is a universal human characteristic, by necessity kleptomaniacs tend to conceal a great many things. Such secrets, or secretive behaviors, are often associated with feelings of shame or embarrassment.

Guilt, Shame and Remorse. Despite behavior that would seem to indicate the contrary, most people suffering from kleptomania feel that stealing is wrong and experience considerable anguish and guilt feelings over their actions.

Addictive Behaviors. In some patients, self defeating, addictive-type behaviors may be common. Relief is virtually always short-lived and, ultimately, self-destructive.

AN ILLEGAL AND EXPENSIVE PROBLEM

What does stealing mean? For kleptomaniacs, "Stealing" seems to be a physical representation or manifestation of a variety of unresolved issues and conflicts. In that respect, kleptomania is not what it appears to be. The issue is not that simple. There are other, important peripheral issues as well. For example, sufferers find themselves in the unique position of being both perpetrators and victims. The possibility exists that a person suffering from kleptomania could be treated with a visit to a prison cell rather than a visit to a psychotherapist—depending on the outcome in the courtroom.

The behavior clearly constitutes an illegal act; at the same time, it is classified as a mental disorder. The potential for misunderstanding is enormous, particularly for those who mistake the disorder as ordinary theft.

I found kleptomania's close relationship with illegality very significant. In fact, it seemed to be sandwiched somewhere between traditional mental illnesses and criminality. Kleptomania is one of the few emotional disorders in which a major behavioral manifestation—theft—constitutes an inherently illegal act. While the tragedy of psychosis or manic-depressive illness is often apparent, there is no inherent criminality associated with these two disorders. The possibility of a depressed person being incarcerated for poor sleeping habits, diminished appetite, or even suicidal feelings is negligible.

On the other hand, individuals suffering from the various impulse disorders share the dubious distinction of imposing their maladaptive behaviors on those around them. The pyromaniac causes loss of property and, often, lives. The pathological gambler squanders the family nest-egg. The explosive individual inflicts physical and emotional violence on others. And, the kleptomaniac steals millions of dollars worth of other people's merchandise. Certainly, the simple desire for knowledge need not be the sole reason for studying kleptomania. A recent article in *The Boston Globe* highlights this issue:

> *"National shoplifting losses amount to $5.1 billion annually, with another $7.5 billion lost to dishonest employees, costing the average United States family $350 each year in higher prices."*

Although the sums lost from kleptomania are but a fraction of these costs, they are large enough to concern the general public. They certainly make kleptomania everyone's business.

But who is doing all the stealing? If kleptomania is a treatable problem, where are all the sufferers? I have become increasingly intrigued by the apparent lack of kleptomaniacs seeking help from mental health practitioners. Past literature declared kleptomania to be rare. There were few patients available for study or treatment. In addition, existing information is often unflattering. Historically, for example, some mental health professionals have "demonized" such patients

by emphasizing what appeared to them to be psychopathic—
or antisocial—traits. Because efforts to treat them had been
met with resistance, they were often compared to common
criminals. Society has traditionally refused to see the kleptomaniac as anything but an odd anomaly, a topic for occasional
gossip—particularly when it involves a notable celebrity's
apprehension for theft. Because of these traditional
approaches, few researchers have concentrated on kleptomania. And, understandably, few people feel secure enough with
current medical practices to come forward to be studied and
treated.

I soon discovered for myself that while some traditional literature would disagree, kleptomania and other forms
of impulsive theft are not rare. Judging from the desperate
letters and phone calls I received after my initial article was
published, it was clear to me that not only did the disorder
exist, but that answers had to be found.

THE INFANCY OF UNDERSTANDING

Even after many years of study and observation on
the subject—and despite my fascination—I still feel only
slightly closer to complete understanding of this maladaptive,
yet self-preserving behavior called kleptomania. At this junc-
ture, I believe the best authorities on the subject are those
whose lives have been turned upside down by their stealing
behaviors.

The inherent information for this book was obtained
from numerous sources. Cases and other important source
material were culled from both my own and others' clinical
records and an exhaustive review of scientific literature. To

define a variety of different characteristics, reported case histories involving the current psychiatric definition of kleptomania were analyzed. To protect the identities of patients, case examples have been altered, but done so in such a manner as to preserve relevance.

The understanding of kleptomania is in its infancy. For sufferers, the need to steal appears to imply that something is missing from their lives. Kleptomaniacs find themselves in the lonely and precarious position of being afflicted with a poorly understood disorder—and nowhere to turn for help. Their families are also dragged into their ongoing nightmare, sometimes unexpectedly forced to provide bail. Confused about who they are and why they are committing certain acts, kleptomaniacs conceal their frustrations only to find it difficult to tolerate their own behaviors. At the same time, society neglects, belittles, and devalues those with the disorder and pays a high financial price for doing so.

Because the disorder is shrouded in secrecy and not well understood, there are many questions. What is kleptomania? What kind of person suffers from it? What can families and loved ones do? What signs and symptoms are associated with the disorder? To more fully understand these complex issues, I will explore a number of different topics. Why does kleptomania appear to be a chronic, episodic disorder? How is it related to other problems of impulse control? How does it relate to other "addictive" type behaviors? I will also review the myths and misconceptions surrounding these sufferers as well as their "secrets" and how they relate to the disorder.

In addition, I will unveil facts about the frequency and personality of those affected. How many kleptomaniacs are there? Are they criminals? Why do they steal? Do they have other difficult-to-manage feelings or behaviors? Who is at risk for developing this disorder? What kinds of life experiences must be present for kleptomania to develop? What are the personality profiles?

Then, to better define and understand kleptomania, we will look at the ways experiences in the lives of all of us resemble those experienced by sufferers of kleptomania. Together, that fine line between "health" and "sickness" can then be explored. In addition, as we look at these lives, I will examine the possible role of early traumatic experiences, deprivation, and loss, and assess the possible role of other impulse problems as well as kleptomania's relationship to criminality and addictions.

Finally, I will explore the value of various treatments, the reactions of patients to them, and their success and failure rates.

This book is for anybody who has stolen out of desperation or for those seeking relief from thoughts or feelings they may not understand. It's also for those who have the impulse to steal but have not yet stolen and for those compromised by other impulse control or addiction problems.

For those who have suffered alone, this book is intended to make them feel less isolated and more at ease. Hopefully, it will inspire sufferers to share their secrets with a caring therapist and will, ideally, enable therapists to become more astute in recognizing this secretive disorder. This book will hopefully also encourage those suffering from kleptomania to enter treatment. Finally, it is a practical guide for others in crisis because of the sufferer's disorder—parents, loved ones, employers, and care givers, like those who have the kleptomania disorder, who do not know how to deal with it and end the silence and loneliness.

Acknowledgments

This book is the product of a variety of important experiences—experiences generated by some very important people. To these individuals I owe a tremendous debt of gratitude:

- To my patients, many of whom put aside their worries and anxieties to graciously provide me with data for this book.

- To my colleagues, who enthusiastically provided me with case histories and support.

- To Tom Gutheil, M.D., who inspired me with his wit, grace and generosity.

- To my agent, Margaret Russell, whose patience and good spirits were much appreciated.

- To Joan Dunphy at New Horizon Press, a special thanks for giving me this opportunity.

- To Hal and Jen, who helped see me through trying times.

- Finally, to my wife, Lori, who gave me space, technical assistance, and encouragement.

Author's Note

This book is based on my research, a thorough study of the available literature and experience counseling patients who have kleptomania, as well as my clients' own real life experiences. Fictitious identities and names have been given to all characters in this book in order to protect individual privacy and some characters are composites.

Introduction

"Stealing was something I had all to myself. Stealing was my friend. It would always keep me company."

                                                    – Paula

Paula, a twenty-six-year-old blonde woman, seems consumed by stealing. After a childhood and young adulthood of misery and loss, she is constantly reminded of the emotional and physical scars of her past by chronic feelings of deprivation, anger, and loneliness. Curiously, she is both soothed and terrified by the knowledge that her misery is often calmed by stealing.

Lara, a thin gray-haired seventy-year-old woman, has already begun to plan her own death. By the time she is readmitted to the hospital for ongoing depression, she has, unfortunately, again taken to stealing, a behavior that has further diminished an already terrible self-image. She has found that the action, strangely enough, tends to relieve some of her emotional pain.

Beth, forty-five, a piquant-faced mother of five children, four sons and one daughter, is financially well off, but without close ties or relationships. Lately she feels constantly alone and as a result has begun to perpetrate a series of petty thefts. Because of a sharp split in her feelings about right and wrong she is growing more deeply disturbed. Although Beth has an almost fanatic desire to be moral and righteous, she is constantly struggling with a self-image that is far from flattering. The acts of theft make her feel sinful and worthless, worthy only of burning in Hell's inferno.

Joe, a burly, balding, thirty-five-year-old professional, told me that he had a lengthy history of stealing books and candy. He had accumulated over thirty-five books this way. He had been apprehended several times.

Susan, a forty-seven-year-old business executive, discusses her secrets with no one. Even her therapist finds it hard to delve into her activities and feelings. Revelation is difficult, and Susan considers her secret bouts of theft too painful to speak of openly. She has had a background of rigid religious upbringing and deep personal convictions. Susan knows and considers it wrong to take from others. At the same time, trauma in her early life has mentally conditioned her to feel that she is entitled to take what she wants.

What a paradox! Good people stealing? Stealing enabling people to feel better? Stealing as a cure, albeit temporary, for suicidal feelings? For Lara, Beth, Susan, Joe, Paula, and others suffering from kleptomania, taking material items from others forms part of the fabric of their lives. Paradoxically eliciting feelings of both distress and relief, their enigmatic disorder—kleptomania—has perplexed generations of researchers and sufferers alike. Exactly what is kleptomania? Is it anything more than a cruel combination of badness, sadness, and madness? Is it sheer thievery? Is it simply "I want" or can it be more closely linked to obsessional behavior? What can be learned about this fascinating but disturbing disorder, which may affect upwards of six out of one thousand people? Most important, what are the substantial obstacles and the best treatments for those who suffer from it?

CHAPTER 1

Myths and Misconceptions

"In addition to being a kleptomaniac, she's also a compulsive liar."
  – From the movie *Teenage Bonnie and Klepto Clyde*

Kleptomania is a secretive disorder. Generally, the traditional lore about kleptomania has proved misleading, flat-out wrong, or irrelevant. Let's look, for instance, at a grade-B movie that exploits the concept of kleptomania for the sole purpose of creating a violent, sensationalistic film.

In *Teenage Bonnie and Klepto Clyde*, Clyde a simple, sexually confused, teenage psychopath steals anything he gets his hands on just to impress the wealthy, vacuous, promiscuous and foul-mouthed Bonnie. Soon the pair is off on a wild cross-country adventure, where their behavior eventually deteriorates into an orgy of thieving and violence designed to heat up their sex lives. Meanwhile, Bonnie's father, the police commissioner, unaware of his daughter's escapades, vows to solve the city's crime wave by having shoplifters, whom he considers "vermin," shot. Not surprisingly, the movie comes to a violent end as the police massacre the duo outside a diner (where Clyde has just stolen a candy bar).

What can we possible learn from this movie? For one thing, it clearly gives us an opportunity to view kleptomania through the eyes of Hollywood. This view, however, does not adequately portray kleptomania. How do I know this? Although the town's ordinarily sleepy tranquility is frequently shattered by Bonnie's sporadic bursts of automatic gunfire, one of the hallmarks of kleptomania, secrecy, is notably absent. Nonetheless, Teenage Bonnie and Klepto Clyde, and films like it, provide us with important points of reference. In fact, the film inadvertently does something helpful; it highlights stereotypical and incorrect thinking about klepto-mania.

Some of the movie's more prominent themes are:

- Stealing as a group activity
- Promiscuity, lust, and sexuality
- Wealth
- Sociopathy
- Criminality
- Violence
- An inability to resist temptation
- Society's anger and misunderstanding
- Unbridled hedonism
- Lack of remorse

Are these characteristic problems really what klepto-mania is all about? Let us take a closer look at some of the real issues.

WHAT WE ALL MUST LEARN ABOUT KLEPTOMANIA

What are kleptomania's "ingredients?" A combination of wealth, fame, sex, and violence? What about guilt and remorse? Do kleptomaniacs take delight in harming others? Do they try to inflict maximum damage? Or are they simply interested in feeling good? It is important to clear our minds of some very mistaken and troublesome myths about the concept of kleptomania. Once free from these misperceptions, we can go on to develop some new ideas about the disorder that are based on fact and reasoned hypotheses rather than on hype and fantasy. First, let us look at some classic myths.

Myth #1: Only the rich and famous suffer from kleptomania.

Newspapers love to print stories about kleptomania. Why not? It is interesting to read about wealthy and famous people taking things they do not need and can obviously afford. Bess Myerson, Hedy Lamar, Manuel Noriega's wife, and many others grab the headlines while the majority of average people with the disorder make only the police blotter. However the rich and famous do not steal because they are rich and famous; rather, kleptomania is a disorder that spares no particular group of people. And although a Hollywood personality caught stealing is more sensational and "newsworthy" than a pharmacist or salesman, it does not mean that only the rich and famous are afflicted.

In truth, the vast majority of those suffering from kleptomania have never been rich or famous. They are not especially recognizable, have no distinguishing marks on their bodies, and do not stand out in a crowd. They are very much like the rest of us. The act of stealing—not the stolen object—signifies the psychological distress, conquest, and reward. Being poor certainly does not preclude this disorder; Kleptomania affects those from all socioeconomic strata.

Myth #2: The kleptomaniac is an eccentric, middle-aged woman who steals because her children have left home.

The once popular notion that kleptomaniacs are middle-aged women who begin stealing in response to their children leaving home—"empty nest syndrome"—simply isn't true. There is nothing eccentric about most kleptomaniacs' appearances or attitudes. In fact, early psychiatric researchers were convinced that kleptomania occurred in the absence of other signs or symptoms typically associated with other mental disorders. They felt that, but for the bizarre stealing behavior, these patients were "normal" in every other way. Hence, they needed some "trigger" to explain the aberration in behavior. They seized on the common belief that women during the menopausal years undergo a midlife crisis as the likely cause. These researchers overlooked evidence indicating that the stealing behavior characteristic of kleptomania may occur in young people and in response to a wide variety of stressors.

Myth #3: The kleptomaniac is a psychopathic criminal who, with fox-like deviousness, steals without remorse.

Just as media reports lead people to misunderstand the relationship between kleptomania and socioeconomic status, historical psychiatric literature has also been guilty of presenting a less than accurate picture—often portraying the

kleptomaniac as a sneaky villain. Indeed, some early psychoanalytic literature suggests that kleptomaniacs are little more
than psychopathic thieves who have little regard for those
around them. Fritz Wittels, an early psychoanalyst, wrote
several papers on the subject during the 1920s and 1940s.
Although much of what he had to say was helpful and interesting, his article *Kleptomania and Other Psychopathic
Crimes* referred to the female shoplifter as "our little lady"
and "a little shoplifter" and categorized them as "criminal
psychopaths"—in my opinion, demeaning and inaccurate
terms. Like everyone else, those suffering from kleptomania
have their own personalities and traits independent of their
stealing behaviors. As we will see, the issue of remorse and
guilt is a complex one. In general, though, the kleptomaniac
has more in common with the depressed and anxious patient
than the anti-social one.

***Myth #4: Kleptomania and ordinary thievery are the same
things.***

Like myth number three, this myth falsely portrays
the kleptomaniac as little more than a common criminal. In the
early years of modern psychiatry—and even more recently—
many practitioners assumed that the origins and characteristics of ordinary stealing for material gain and kleptomania
were identical. What has often been called "kleptomania" is
not kleptomania at all, but some other type of stealing.

A recent article illustrates this point. The author was
discussing kleptomania in a young woman. The woman stole
only items that she liked and which had value for her. Her
stealing was planned in advance and she used the items she

stole. Such behavior should have precluded a finding of kleptomania in her case, but she was nonetheless improperly diagnosed as a kleptomaniac. A misdiagnosis such as this, damages and dilutes the legitimacy of the disorder and hurts those really suffering from it. Because of this confusion, kleptomaniacs are sometimes considered to be thieving psychopaths, and thieving psychopaths are sometimes considered to be kleptomaniacs. The distinction between common theft and kleptomania must be recognized if we are ever to come to grips with either.

Myth #5: Kleptomaniacs are sexually wild and have orgasms when they steal.

The issue of sexuality and kleptomania is a complex one. Where does this false myth come from? Early psychiatric literature is one of the culprits, with writers making frequent references to kleptomania and sex in the same breath. Their prejudices have survived for years. In fact, current literature and articles continue this myth by labeling kleptomaniacs as sexually "wild" and making references to the kleptomaniac experiencing sexual arousal while stealing. The idea of this link between kleptomania and wild sexual behavior may be interesting, but is probably atypical, occurring only in rare cases.

Aside from misleading literature, kleptomania may also be inappropriately labeled a sexual disorder because of the confusion stemming from the concept of "fetishism." A fetish is an object that is used to stimulate sexual excitement or arousal. There are foot fetishes, tomato fetishes, shoe fetishes—unlimited possibilities. Past literature has suggested that stolen objects have been used as fetishes.

However, fetishism and kleptomania are two completely different disorders. One does not need to be a kleptomaniac to have a fetish and one does not need to be a fetishist to be a kleptomaniac. To appreciate the unfortunate blurring of issues of objective sexual perversion and kleptomania, one needs only to look at *The Encyclopedia of Unusual Sexual Practices* by Brenda Love to see a complete page devoted to stealing. In reality, kleptomania doesn't belong in a textbook of unusual sexual practices. More likely, kleptomania's relationship to sex has more to do with symbolic, rather than orgasmic, representations of sexuality.

Myth #6: Kleptomaniacs are completely at the mercy of the disorder, are mentally ill, and are unable to meet the ordinary demands of life.

The term "mental illness" means different things to different people. In psychiatry it generally refers to someone who has a very severe disorder of thought, mood, perception, orientation, or memory, and who is greatly impaired, with serious difficulties in exercising proper judgment. Such mentally ill sufferers find it nearly impossible to meet the ordinary demands of life. I have found in my experience that kleptomaniacs do not display the signs or symptoms that are common with the mentally ill. For the most part, I tend to refer to kleptomaniacs as having a "disorder" or a "disturbance" rather than a "mental illness." I also hold people suffering from kleptomania accountable for their behavior, for reasons that will be discussed later on. However, certainly most can work and are not substantially impaired. And, most of them successfully meet the demands of life and are often hardworking and productive.

Given the widespread currency of these myths and the many problems understanding this disorder, it should come as no surprise that the term 'kleptomania' (Greek for "stealing madness" or "stealing insanity") is actually a misnomer. Kleptomania encompasses far more than merely "stealing" and is hardly an illness of "mad" or "insane" proportions as the translation of the word implies. And, it is little wonder that most kleptomaniacs don't want to disclose their affliction and are often quite ambivalent about receiving help for their problem.

CHAPTER 2

Misunderstanding and Misidentity

"There's a little larceny in everyone."

– Anonymous

Why is kleptomania so poorly understood? I once asked a dozen guests at a party how many of them had ever stolen anything. Eleven uncomfortably responded that they had. Then, with caution, each revealed his or her individual tale of theft, the telling of which seemed to elicit feelings of both fear and fascination.

Stealing, or even mental illness, hits most people very close to home. To protect themselves from uncomfortable feelings, most people seek to distance themselves—physically, spiritually, and emotionally—from the mentally ill. The notion of segregation seems simple and straightforward: put people who seem so different in a different place. Could it be that what bothers us aren't the differences, but the things we have in common with those affected by illness?

Some uninhibited psychiatric patients suffering from acute severe manic states, for example, act hypersexually, spend money they don't have, and are clinically euphoric. In rare cases, angry psychiatric patients may injure or even kill those who anger them.

The ways in which we interpret or make sense of our environment are the products of millions of stimuli and experiences throughout our lives. Given the proper biological and environmental circumstances, people under great stress may be inclined to react or respond in a more pathological or poorly adaptive way to a given situation. Given the scope of human experience, we have all been fleetingly mentally impaired at one time or another. Most of us manage to pull ourselves away from pathology and redirect ourselves back to health. Here is a brief list of some of the ways in which healthy people transiently experience the kinds of signs and symptoms that are persistently present in mentally ill persons:

- The experience of déjà vu, in which we seem to recreate past feelings or events;
- Nightmares in which we experience hallucinations, paranoia, and delusions;
- Temporary depression or suicidal feelings;
- Overwhelming anxiety at a moment of stress;
- Elements of post-traumatic stress disorder during moments of uncomfortable remembrances;
- Manic excitement caused by fatigue, where we impulsively overspend or become so excited about something that we become energized and can't sleep;
- Pathological jealousy where we may be momentarily convinced that our partner is being unfaithful;

- Sociopathy and explosiveness where we may stretch the truth, kick the dog, keep change not due to us, or scream at our children;
  - Overeating or undereating when stressed;
  - Obsessive-compulsive behavior such as repeated hand-washing when we feel we have been contaminated by something.

Mercifully, such lapses into "mental illness" end quickly. That we do not develop a mental illness or disturbance is a matter of balance, tolerance, genetics, and the ability to use our health to recover. In general, our experiences represent not the true mental disorders that others possess but degrees of all our past experiences that make us who we are. As we will later see, a person suffering from kleptomania engages in behavior that is most likely an attempt to soothe affective (mood) and anxiety states. The rest of us tend to employ other techniques to accomplish this and feel worlds away from being impaired. That separation, however, may be more of degree than of kind, and it is crucial for all parties to realize that stealing is a far less foreign behavior than we are all led to believe.

The fine line that exists between "madness" and "sanity" is not always clear. But what about theft? Are kleptomaniacs mad or sane? As we will discover, kleptomaniacs steal in order to relieve sadness and anxiety. What actions do we take to relieve those same anxieties? Most of us find other ways to alleviate our tension than stealing. We do not take something that does not belong to us. However, many of us are aware of people who do.

• Ena, an office worker with whom I spoke, initially laughed at the word kleptomania. Then she remembered that she had an aunt who, when visiting, used to excuse herself from the dinner table to go through her nieces' and nephews' rooms. Although she was a relative, the aunt often stole small items from them that she didn't need.

• Joe, a burly, balding, thirty-five-year-old professional, told me that he had a lengthy history of stealing books and candy. He had accumulated over thirty-five books this way. He had been apprehended several times.

• Phillip, a distinguished college professor, was arrested for stealing a textbook shortly after leaving the campus bookstore.

• Bertha, a fifty-two-year-old woman, stole money from the government by overstating the amount of deductions legally due to her on her federal income tax returns.

• Meg, a thirty-two-year-old mother, while shopping had the habit of picking up and eating food in the grocery store before she arrived at the checkout counter. In this way, she consumed food and did not have to pay for it.

• Martin, a young, neurotic psychiatrist, noticed that he had accumulated dozens of unused pens and pads of paper. He realized that he had been taking them from work.

• Jennifer, a thirty-six-year-old nutritionist, stole money from a retail store by failing to notify the cashier that she had received too much change from her purchase.

In an article which appeared in *People* magazine several years ago, a question is asked: "How big a Paul McCartney fan is MTV's Martha Quinn, thirty-two, who interviewed the former Beatle a year ago?" She stated: "He had been drinking some tea during the interview, and, after it was over, he got up and left. I went over, looked in the cup, and the tea was, like, half a cup still there. I picked it up and drank it. I didn't care if I got a disease—I wanted to. If it was from Paul McCartney, that'd be okay." Quinn, who has been with MTV for most of its ten-year history, reveals that she stole the cup and saucer. "I haven't washed it to this day. It still has remains of his tea in it. And I have the spoon, too."

For those of us who do not suffer from kleptomania, the idea of any type of stealing may appear completely repugnant, and we may wish to distance ourselves emotionally from such behavior. Actually, stealing is an almost universal developmental behavior—one that the majority of us have willingly participated in at one time or another. As children or adolescents, we often measured our social successes in terms of ownership and frequently wanted to take what others had. A quick glance at two-year-olds trying to play with the same toy will soon convince us of this. Stealing away objects from each other does not end in infancy, however. A virtual teenage rite of passage is stealing with our peers—we even accept dares to steal from stores or from each other.

As we get older, our methods become more sophisticated. Cheating on income taxes, receiving and keeping extra change from a purchase, or even eating food in the grocery store on the way to the checkout counter are but a few of the many ways we learn to deprive others and gratify ourselves. If the above behaviors do not sound familiar, then consider that some of us end up with dozens of pens, paper clips, and other items presumably taken from the workplace. There is a spectrum of thievery that begins with "accidental theft" (paper clips and such) and continues on through tax fraud and other willful acts of theft. The line between unwitting and willful theft is not at all clear. Regardless of such nuances, there is much truth in the saying, "There's a little larceny in everyone."

This observation has led me to "steal" part of a phrase from Sigmund Freud's book, *The Psychopathology of Everyday Life* which points out and explains the various forms of pathology present in each of us as we go about our business during the day. The phrase I use, "the kleptomania of everyday life," is in no way meant to imply that we are all kleptomaniacs or even that our stealing is related to klepto-mania (although our questionable habits may be subject to a kind of sliding scale of pathology which, in times of stress, may enable us to do things we ordinarily might never consider doing). Admittedly, these examples do not represent all of the kinds of stealing seen in kleptomania, but they do show that we have some things in common with those we so unthink-ingly have pushed away. Perhaps if we examine the preva-lence of the disorder we can get a better perspective on the malady and how it affects people, some of them very much like us, every day.

IS THERE SAFETY IN NUMBERS?

In addition to quantifying the problem of kleptomania, at least insofar as possible, another advantage of learning how common it is lies in the possible treatment opportunities such knowledge may open for people. For example, if those with the disorder realized that others suffer from the same spectrum of symptoms, they might feel more relaxed and more comfortable about coming forward to seek mental health services. Admittedly, reliably estimating how many people suffer from kleptomania is a very difficult task, but it seems likely that the sufferers are in reasonably good company.

Traditionally, kleptomania has been considered to be quite rare. Many think it is a mere occasional anomaly while others suggest that it does not exist at all. There are many reasons for kleptomania's reportedly low prevalence rates, so we may do well to take a look at those most likely to benefit from a more accurate assessment of its prevalence and to suffer from its inaccurate portrayal.

Because people suffering from kleptomania seldom come forward for treatment, society views those who are occasionally apprehended as oddities. Just because sufferers keep a low profile, however, does not mean the disorder is a rare one. We should remember that people with eating disorders rarely come forward for treatment either, but this does not mean such disorders are uncommon.

For instance, while studying the reported cases of people suffering from kleptomania or disorders approximating kleptomania, I noticed something very interesting and unusual. Unlike people with mental illnesses or other emotional disorders who normally seek out help or whose signs and symptoms are very obvious, eighty-five percent of kleptomaniacs came to the attention of a mental health professional only after they had been referred by way of the court system.

This suggests that unless they are apprehended, most kleptomaniacs will not come forward voluntarily. Because most who steal don't get caught, this implies that the vast majority of sufferers may not come to the attention of mental health professionals and may very well be grossly underrepresented in previous prevalence statistics. My own personal experience has been that people harboring the secret of kleptomania who do seek out treatment will almost never come to a mental health professional requesting help for that malady.

They will invariably ask for help with other symptoms such as depression or anxiety and will reveal the stealing behavior only much later, if at all. In a later chapter, we'll take a look at some estimated prevalence rates.

IT LOOKS LIKE KLEPTOMANIA, BUT IT'S NOT

Let's face it! There is a lot of theft going on in the world. How much of it is kleptomania and how much of it is just plain stealing? Let us explore this world of stealing a bit more closely.

Ordinary Theft: Ordinary stealing occurs when an item is taken solely for profit or personal use. It may be out of conscious vengeance or anger, or it may arise simply because the person wants something and decides to take it. Such robbery may serve many purposes, for example, to support a drug habit or simply to make money, as with professional thieves. Prisons are full of people who "break and enter" in order to steal. The majority of thefts occur through ordinary stealing. It is distinguished from kleptomania because the act is generally *not* impulsive—it is more generally preplanned and often done in conjunction with others. Furthermore, it is *not* done to reduce an increasing sense of tension, and it *is* done for monetary gain.

A twenty-two-year-old male, incarcerated for violation of probation, told me that he was recently arrested for shoplifting, and that he felt that he suffered from kleptomania. He told me that he had stolen a coat that he did not want. When I asked him why he took the coat, he smiled and said that he was with a group of friends and that he had stolen the coat because all of his friends were doing it.

Malingering: Malingering occurs when people pretend to have an emotional disorder when in fact they do not. Sometimes those accused of ordinary theft pretend to suffer from kleptomania. This is seen most frequently in a legal or courtroom setting where the alleged perpetrator of a crime feigns kleptomania in order to be adjudged not guilty of a crime. Kleptomania has been recognized as a potential source of malingering for over 100 years; for example, as long ago as 1853, a psychiatrist, Dr. Duncan, discussed kleptomania as grounds for an insanity plea but also pointed out that those accused of theft might attempt to feign the disorder. Today, it's still possible for shoplifters, addicts, and others to try to protect themselves by pretending to be kleptomaniacs, but if we carefully review the disorder's diagnostic criteria and closely examine the would-be malingerer's behavior and intentions towards the stolen objects, we will generally be able to uncover inconsistencies in their stories.

Conduct Disorder: This is a disorder of childhood or adolescence characterized by, among other things, stealing. However, there are numerous other associated symptoms such as setting fires, cruelty to animals or people, forced sexual activity, and destruction of property. The old phrase "juvenile delinquent" was often used to describe such unruly, cruel, and destructive youths. In determining whether kleptomania exists in cases involving these disturbed—and disturbing—youths, attention must be paid to their other associated symptoms and absence of the kinds of signs and symptoms common in kleptomania.

Antisocial Personality Disorder: This disorder, diagnosed when a person is at least eighteen, can involve stealing but is also characterized by the other kinds of behaviors seen in conduct disorder. The term "antisocial personality disorder" replaces the old term "psychopath." Other associated symptoms include lying, cruelty, physical aggression, and lack of remorse. As in conduct disorder, attention must be paid to the person's other associated symptoms and the absence of the kinds of signs and symptoms common in kleptomania.

Mania: Mania is a major mental illness characterized by rapid speech, agitation, lack of need for sleep, elevated mood, grandiosity, and extremely poor judgment. Because there is an alteration in the way these people may think and act, stealing can occur.

Jeffrey was a twenty-three-year-old man with a history of mania. He would become extremely agitated and slept only three hours per night. He seemed euphoric and could not stop talking. His mood was so elated and his attitude so grandiose that he believed he could both buy objects well in excess of his financial capabilities and could take anything he wanted from stores.

Because of mania's associated symptoms, it is generally easy to tell the difference between it and kleptomania.

Schizophrenia: Schizophrenia, like mania, is a major mental illness. It is characterized by delusions (fixed false beliefs) and hallucinations (hearing voices when no one is present). Patients, in response to such hallucinations and delusions, can steal and engage in a variety of other odd or disruptive behaviors.

Stacey was a twenty-year-old woman who often heard voices of other people. She also felt that demons were in her body. The voices told Stacey that if she did not take clothes from her roommate's drawer, she would be sent to Hell.

To differentiate between kleptomania and stealing in response to a psychotic illness like schizophrenia, mental health workers must be careful to note the bizarre nature of the patient's thoughts and behavior.

Organic Mental Disorders: People with organic mental disorders such as drug-induced confusion, senile dementia, or Alzheimer's Disease may often fail to pay for items they pick up in stores or elsewhere. These people generally are confused or have poor memories, making this kind of stealing easy to distinguish from kleptomania.

Paul, a sixty-seven-year-old retired school teacher with no past psychiatric or criminal record, was arrested for a series of bizarre behaviors. He had been setting fires and had also been caught stealing furniture from his next door neighbor's home. He would take large pieces of furniture and store them on his front porch, in full view of the community. Upon questioning, Paul was disoriented but admitted that he had been using excessive amounts of blood pressure medication. His bizarre behavior stopped after cessation of the medication.

As can be seen, people suffering from kleptomania have some very specific signs and symptoms that differentiate them from those with disorders that can sometimes look like kleptomania. Despite the relative ease with which we can diagnostically dismiss most cases of stealing that do not adhere to kleptomania's diagnostic criteria, it is not always so straightforward.

WHEN DIAGNOSIS IS A JUDGMENT CALL

Given all of this information, one would think that

making the diagnosis of kleptomania would be fairly easy. After all, the criteria seem well elucidated and unambiguous. In real life, however, when we try to make a diagnosis of kleptomania, a complex, secretive and poorly understood disorder, we are frequently confronted with a set of signs or symptoms that may either fall short of the "official" criteria or markedly exceed them. Sometimes it's because reliable data is lacking or because we have only an incomplete history, but often it stems simply from the ambiguous nature of the disorder. What, for example, would we call a person who steals things he or she does not need and could easily afford, but experiences no sense of irresistible impulse? What do we call someone whose stealing is nonsensical and irresistible but who is unable to confirm a sense of building tension or relief? What is a person who often steals items he or she doesn't need or regularly use? Ambiguity and uncertainty go with the territory.

One of the problems facing those of us in this field is uncertainty. Unlike other medical specialties that can rely on laboratory examinations or physical signs and symptoms to determine a diagnosis, those of us in the mental health field must rely on factors far more elusive and subjective.

Worse still, citing the lack of "pure" cases of kleptomania (that is, patients who conform exactly to all the diagnostic criteria outlined in the *Diagnostic and Statistical Manual* or *DSM-IV Manual*), some researchers have rejected outright the very concept of kleptomania. There is, however, a problem inherent in the demand for a "pure" case of kleptomania; in psychiatry, you'll almost never find a "pure" anything. Like anything else in life, the fluidity of the human condition must be taken into account. People's behaviors result from thousands of life experiences and a merging of long-standing character or personality traits and affective states. The signs and symptoms of illness track a complex interaction between biology, character, and environment, and they cannot be reduced to a short formulation that can be applied consistently to one patient after another.

It is my belief that the stated criteria alone are not sufficient to diagnose a case satisfactorily. In kleptomania, a study of the person's attitudes and the intense affective (emotional) states that drive the behavior is the only way to clarify those cases that appear unclear or contradictory to the stated guidelines. It seems that some kleptomaniacs can evince signs and symptoms both consistent with and inconsistent with the diagnostic criteria at various times in their lives. People may take items for a variety of reasons and in many different ways. For example, what about magazines a person takes to read, but which are not needed and pile up unused? Sufferers, families, and therapists must all remember that the written criteria are only *guidelines*; they are invaluable but they are not infallible. Ambiguity does not negate the existence of the disorder, and we should resist the temptation to throw the baby out with the bathwater in those cases where the facts do not precisely mirror the established criteria.

CHAPTER 3

What is Kleptomania?

"The recurrent failure to resist impulses to steal items even though the items are not needed for personal use or their monetary value."

— DSM-IV

Rule of thumb holds that if it walks like a duck, quacks like a duck, and swims like a duck—it's a duck! Recognizing kleptomania, however, is nowhere near as easy, not for those who suffer from it, not for their families, and not for society at large.

However, some salient characteristics of kleptomania are often tipoffs that the stealing in question is more than theft. When she first came to see me, Susan, a forty-seven-year-old woman, suffered from a variety of emotional problems. She had recently been discharged from a psychiatric hospital after having been sent there by her therapist because he was no longer able to help her deal with her many conflicts. Susan was treated with medication for depressive episodes, but she chose to reveal virtually nothing about herself or her personal life during her therapy sessions. She was guarded and secretive, preferring instead to shield herself from others, even those who might be of assistance to her. It was many years before Susan was ready to reveal her biggest secret.

Eventually it became clear that Susan feared that her repetitive theft of items which she did not need and could easily afford to buy was apt to lead to her arrest and incarceration. Despite these fears, she did finally reveal that her home contained dozens of unopened packages of stockings, none of which fit her, cans of vegetables she does not care for, and some inexpensive objects that she does not need but takes and uses. Susan's stealing behavior, which feels quite irresistible to her, brings her relief from stress and tension. Although she feels entitled to steal, she expresses remorse about the thefts. Even so, she has never sought treatment on her own, preferring instead to keep this behavior and other things a secret. Like most who suffer from kleptomania, Susan did not come to the hospital or to her therapist in order to receive help for her stealing behavior. Instead, she was seeking help for numerous other complaints. All of this is consonant with a diagnosis of kleptomania, but, first, exactly what criteria are needed to make such a diagnosis?

DIAGNOSING KLEPTOMANIA

Kleptomania has had a checkered history of definition. Today, the formal diagnostic criteria for kleptomania can be found in the *Diagnostic and Statistical Manual*, or *DSM-IV*. This manual is used by mental health practitioners to transmit to each other the general characteristics of patients they may be treating. Although it is supposed to act only as a guide, the manual is called on more and more frequently to provide definitive diagnostic criteria for given disorders. *DSM-IV* considers kleptomania to be a disorder of impulse and control and defines it as:

> *". . . the recurrent failure to resist impulses to steal items even though the items are not needed for personal use or their monetary value. The individual experiences a rising subjective sense of tension before the theft and feels pleasure, gratification or relief while committing the theft. The stealing is not committed to express anger or vengeance, is not done in response to a delusion or hallucination, and is not better accounted for by conduct disorder, a manic episode or antisocial personality disorder. The objects are stolen despite the fact that they are typically of little value to the individual, who could have afforded to pay for them and often gives them away or discards them. Occasionally, the individual with this disorder may hoard the stolen objects or surreptitiously return them. Although individuals with this disorder will generally avoid stealing when immediate arrest is probable (e.g., in full view of a police officer), they usually do not preplan the thefts or fully take into account the chances of apprehension. The stealing is done without assistance from, or collaboration with, others."*

The following criteria must be met in order for a patient to be "officially" diagnosed with kleptomania:

1. Recurrent failure to resist impulses to steal objects that are not needed for personal use or for their monetary value.
2. Increasing sense of tension immediately before committing the theft.
3. Pleasure, gratification, or relief at the time of committing the theft.
4. Stealing not committed to express anger or vengeance and not in response to a delusion or hallucination.
5. Stealing behavior that cannot be better accounted for by another disorder, e.g., conduct disorder, a manic episode, or antisocial personality disorder.

Even though these criteria appear complete and reasonable, they are by no means the final word. There are those, for example, who consider kleptomania to be a symptom of some other psychiatric disorder. In this book, we will try to avoid the tangled diagnostic difficulties by *considering the essence of this disorder to be the apparent absurdity of the act*. What is stolen is *not* needed. Most types of theft have material gain as their rationale; the thefts of kleptomaniacs do not. Generally speaking, what gain there is comes from the relief of stress obtained through the theft of unneeded objects.

THE *DSM-IV* DIAGNOSTIC CRITERIA: CLARIFICATIONS AND APPLICATIONS

Diagnostic criteria for kleptomania, like criteria for

other mental disorders, evolved over time. Perhaps reflecting an ongoing ambivalence about the very existence of klepto-mania, the authors of the *Diagnostic and Statistical Manual* (*DSM-I*), published in 1952, included kleptomania only as a supplementary term and not as an established diagnostic entity. Researchers obviously were not yet convinced that kleptomania was a disorder in and of itself, the consensus being that the disorder was perhaps a symptom or part of some other psychiatric diagnosis. The diagnosis was entirely left out of the next generation of psychiatric diagnostic manuals. It eventually found its way back into the manual with both *DSM-III* and the revised edition, *DSM-IIIR*. The *DSM-IV*, today's manual, maintains kleptomania's status as an independent diagnosis.

Kleptomania is now considered a disorder of impulse control and has been so classified in the last two manuals. What does the word "impulse" mean? What does it imply? We need to examine the use of words in these criteria more closely to appreciate just what the professional literature con-siders kleptomania to be. A good place to start is a careful review of each of the criteria.

A.) *Recurrent failure to resist impulses to steal objects not needed for personal use or their monetary value.*

Let's break this first diagnostic criterion down into two components. First, "the recurrent failure to resist impulses to steal objects." One of the defining hallmarks of the impulse disorders, of which kleptomania is but one, is that the person is unable to fight off a repetitive impulse. An impulse is a sudden, most likely unreasoning, determination to perform an act of some sort. In impulse disorders, the "impulse" is to engage in a potentially injurious activity. In the case of kleptomania, the "injurious" activity is, of course, stealing. The following vignettes highlight the unremitting and seemingly irresistible impulse to steal that characterizes kleptomaniacs.

In describing the case of a thirty-year-old woman, Gauthier and Pellerin noted that "During the initial interview she complained of difficulties in controlling her urges to steal, which occurred whenever she went shopping. She admitted acting upon these urges on almost every occasion."

In another example, one author, in describing kleptomania in a forty-year-old woman, states, "At least several times a week, in response to irresistible impulses, she would steal minor items from retail stores. . . . This pattern was unremitting over the years."

Gudjonsson, in writing about a compulsive shoplifter whose behavior approximated kleptomania, presented the case of a middle-aged woman. In discussing the intensity of the drive to steal, the author reports that "The urge to shoplift had grown stronger over the years and the patient reported finding it increasingly difficult to resist it. She had five convictions for shoplifting, the last conviction resulting in a suspended prison sentence."

Another author, in describing the behavior of a middle-aged woman stated, "Once the urge to shoplift was clearly formulated, the impulse to steal was in the majority of instances irresistible."

These examples underscore the repetitive, impulsive need to steal as well as the hazards involved. The notion of irresistibility seems to imply an almost addictive-like phenomenon. We will discuss this interesting notion in a later chapter, but, as can be seen here, the level of need is so great that at times it appears to be stronger than the desire to avoid arrest.

The second part of this criterion, namely, the theft of "objects not needed for personal use or their monetary value" deals with the apparent absurdity of the act because it asserts that the kleptomaniac does not profit monetarily from the theft and can easily afford to purchase the items instead of stealing them. Further emphasizing the absurd or futile nature of the act is the fact that many kleptomaniacs simply hoard, return, or even discard the items they have put themselves at such risk to acquire. The following vignettes illustrate these points.

Elizur & Jaffe, in describing theft by a twenty-five-year-old woman, stated that the patient "later took objects of little value (prizes, pens, etc.) from her girlfriends."

In another example, H. Davis wrote of a woman who had been convicted of stealing a blouse which was neither the correct size nor needed by her.

McElroy and colleagues reported the case of a woman who "first developed an irrepressible impulse to steal clothes after walking out of a department store wearing a pair of slacks that she had tried on in a changing room. . . . She atoned for her thefts by leaving the clothes at charity collection centers."

Medlicott found that "A married man of forty-seven years had taken and hoarded articles from his employer. He was entitled to more goods than he stole, and at the time his hidden cache was discovered he had loaned his employer a considerable sum of money."

McConaghy and Blaszczynski cited the case of a thirty-nine-year-old woman who "stole items of clothing for herself and her children, which were often of no use, for example, because they did not fit. Mainly, she took stockings which she did not need as she said she had cupboards full of stolen stockings."

One woman, who was smuggled out of Poland in a cheese sack, settled in America and worked in a factory for many years. During that time she stole thousands of pills (including analgesics as well as pills used to combat menstrual pain), bandages, and plastic bags, which she never used. She distributed the items to her relatives who seldom required the items. The extent of her thievery was so great that piles of unused goods remained years after her death.

Paula, a young woman we will meet later, stole combs, brushes, and perfume from her friends. She also took shoes that she never wore and, as a school girl, stole lunches which she threw away.

These examples illustrate the apparent nonsensical nature of the act, that is, taking things one does not need, does not use, or could easily afford. Although the act is seemingly absurd, we will later explore the possible reasons for this peculiar behavior. For now we need to ask what kinds of feelings and emotional states precede the stealing behavior seen in the examples above. The second diagnostic criterion gives us a few hints.

B.) *Increasing sense of tension immediately before committing the theft.*

Like people exhibiting other impulse disorders, those suffering from kleptomania experience an intense emotion or feelings of high tension just prior to the impulsive act. This feeling of tension may take the form of stress, nervousness, or anxiety. Typically, descriptions of increasing "sense of tension" involve statements like "She felt mounting tension prior to the act of theft" or "mounting tension if the urge was resisted."

Or as Paula tells us, "I don't think about it before I take. If I see something, I automatically go for it without thinking. I get palpitations and start to sweat. I didn't have to take the lunch as if I had nothing to eat, but I couldn't stop myself. It happens so quickly. It's never planned. All of a sudden I'm doing it—my heart's racing and it's over. It happens so quickly."

How then is this increasing sense of tension or anxiety relieved? Although we will be discussing this symptom relief mechanism later on, the next criterion helps to at least partially answer this question:

C.) *Pleasure, gratification, or relief at the time of committing the theft.*

This criterion treats one of the most interesting observations about kleptomania—that the tension built up just prior to stealing is discharged by the act itself. For patients suffering from kleptomania, the act of stealing appears to give them a sense of gratification, well being, or relief from symptoms of stress or anxiety. The following brief vignettes highlight the intense gratification or relief of tension brought on by theft.

One woman felt "a brief period of ease and self-satisfaction"; another experienced a "rush" after stealing; and yet another: "After leaving the shop with the stolen goods, she experienced a distinct relief of anxiety which gave her a strong feeling of well-being."

My own research reveals that the majority of kleptomaniacs experience either relief of tension or both relief of tension and pleasure. The notion of the kleptomaniac deriving a particular kind of sexual pleasure from theft has been of great interest over the years. We will be looking more closely at this relief technique later.

D.) *The stealing is not committed to express anger or vengeance and is not in response to a delusion or hallucination.*

There are, of course, many different kinds of theft. The *DSM-IV* is quite specific, though, in its determination *not* to let "reactive" stealing—revenge stealing or stealing to "pay someone back" for their real or perceived wrongs—be mistaken for kleptomania. In other words, depriving someone of his belongings because of rage, anger, or a desire to retaliate for some actual or perceived wrong precludes diagnosing that act as kleptomania. No matter how intense or irresistible the desire is, as long as the act is preplanned and consciously motivated, it is not kleptomania. This is not to say that such anger or vengeance cannot be unconscious—a point we will examine later. Finally, theft in response to a delusion or hallucination does not qualify as kleptomania.

E.) *The stealing is not better accounted for by conduct disorder, a manic episode, or antisocial personality disorder.*

People carrying diagnoses of Antisocial Personality Disorder who steal do so for a variety of reasons not consistent with the stealing seen in kleptomania. There may be some overlap between this criterion and the third criterion. For example, people with histories of antisocial behavior may steal for material gain or profit or because they are angered or enraged and consciously wish to deprive someone or some organization of goods. There are, of course, people whose vocation is thievery. A clear example of this type of stealing occurred during a recent crime wave in the Boston area, where professional thieves used specially lined bags to keep the stores' theft sensors from detecting the stolen merchandise as it was carried out. Of vital importance here is the pre-planned nature of the act as well as the fact that the stealing was done in a group. Moreover, the stealing had material gain for its goal.

CHAPTER 4

Families in Crisis

"I can understand my sister's refusal to consider help, but I fear what lies ahead for her."

— Carla

Most of us see illness, disease, or disorder as being limited only to the individual affected. For example, if a person suffers from schizophrenia, we are not likely to infer that the person's mother, father, sister, or brother suffers from it as well. There is much evidence, however, that illnesses—particularly emotional disorders—exist not in isolation but in conjunction with, or more accurately perhaps, in turmoil with their surroundings. A patient suffering from schizophrenia may cause his or her family great emotional distress simply because the illness is so grave. Likewise, the families and friends of a kleptomaniac clearly suffer along with the patient. What is true for patients is often true for members of their families or their loved ones—especially as it relates to the depth of suffering and sense of isolation. For such families, despair is often the only available response to a behavior that destroys. Both family and patient are caught in a terrible dilemma, wanting to find help and shunning it at the same time.

THE DESPAIR OF THE FAMILY

It would be hard to overstate the shock experienced by most families of kleptomaniacs. Imagine a respectable, hardworking father who is suddenly called down to a grimy precinct house to find his daughter lined up with crackheads, drug dealers, prostitutes, pickpockets, scam artists, and all the other denizens of America's criminal justice system. Suddenly a family whose most heinous crime has been an illegal parking ticket must now learn a new vocabulary: "docket," "probation," "remanded," and a host of other terms they've only seen or heard through television shows. The father may find himself saying, "Officer, I don't know why she took those blouses. I would have bought them for her," in a cry of rage and incomprehension. Then to himself, *How can I face the family? My friends?*

Families of kleptomaniacs can scarcely avoid becoming involved in the problem. Often they must bear the shock and shame of these confrontations by themselves, either because they don't know where to turn or because they can't bring themselves to admit the situation openly. They are forced to keep a very powerful and painful secret, and this complicity in covering up the patient's behavior takes its toll. They agonize over and fear for their loved one's behavior, which they see as irresponsible and incomprehensible.

Not only are they fearful, but they find themselves humiliated again and again as repeated arrests stigmatize the family and make all efforts at covering up increasingly futile. Again and again they ask themselves, "How could this happen? Why did this happen?" Often they dredge up old wounds and painful memories from the past in a search for answers. If the opportunity should present itself, they are eager to share these with someone they feel can understand and help. Carla, a woman who wrote to me on behalf of her sister, tells the family story:

> "I have a sister with a problem and I believe it is an effect of an abusive childhood. My sister, Ann, is older than I. Our mother is a now-deceased manic-depressive; father, also deceased, was an alcoholic. My sister was a quiet, fearful child, lacking confidence in herself, and, as the first sibling, felt 'responsible' for the unhappiness of my mother. Our mother had been generally depressed during our earlier childhood, had a complete breakdown when Ann was thirteen, and then began to have regular manic episodes. I am told that, on her wedding night, she was found in a 'catatonic trance,' and therefore I believe that her illness was well developed by the time my sister and I were born.
>
> "There were many terrifying and sometimes violent events during our childhood, when our father came home drunk. I was aware of several incidents of 'minor' sexual abuse (looking, perhaps a 'quick touch') from our mother's brothers, and some inappropriate hugging from our father. My sister seemed to have very little awareness of this, however.

"My mother would frequently steal 'little things,' like mirrors which, back then, generally came with a woman's purse, or perhaps the scarf or belt that came with a dress. She would always rationalize these thefts. She was arrested once. The interesting thing about this otherwise agonizing event was that she was obviously in the manic phase of her illness when it happened, but the incident brought her into a depression immediately.

"Our mother essentially took Ann's childhood away. My mother cried that she didn't want to be alone, and my sister would often give up whatever plans she might have made in order to stay with her. This burden was not really shared by me; I tried to be out as much as possible. This is, of course, my guilt. My sister couldn't leave our mother crying and depressed, would stay with her, and wound up baby-sitting for a sleeping adult. My sister didn't go out on many dates, although she was quite attractive, until she was about seventeen. At eighteen, she had a daughter out of wedlock. She raised her in our home, until she married, when this wonderful child was four years old.

"My sister is an intelligent, hardworking, loving, and stubborn woman. She is fiercely loyal to her family. She seems to have no problem casting off outside people once they have offended her. She has expressed feelings of inadequacy to me. She has said that, although she knows she did everything possible for our mother, she still feels that she should have done more.

"In terms of my sister's stealing, I am aware of her being caught four times in the past eight years. The strain is taking its toll on Ann's husband, who is in the medical field and is thus quite visible in the community. He is not sure that their marriage will endure unless my sister gets some help. So far, there has been no publicity. The items taken are usually food from the supermarket. I have discussed the material from your articles with her. She *is* aware of feelings of depression prior to these events. She feels that understanding the problem will help her overcome it. I don't share that belief; nothing is ever that simple. However, after watching our mother go through all those years of dulling medication, horrifying shock treatments, and more, Ann refuses to even consider taking any medication. She feels the best therapy would be her own understanding of the problem. Ann said she feels 'ill' at the very thought of medication or therapy at this time. I can understand my sister's refusal to consider help, but I fear what lies ahead for her."

This story is important because it reveals how both patients and their families suffer and worry alone. It's also a good example of just how persistent the behavior can be and how tough it is for patients to defeat it on their own. Finally, it demonstrates that people suffering from kleptomania are not monsters—they may be hardworking, loyal, empathic, and intelligent.

In such a complicated situation, the sufferers have their own sets of issues, of course, but it is their friends, family, or loved ones who must live in the shadow of their behavior. I have received many calls from frustrated, hurt, and bewildered parents who simply cannot understand what is happening to their children and who are unable to find help for themselves or their troubled offspring. They feel as alone as the patient, and they are often equally traumatized by the disruptive behavior. Discussed below are some of the more common thoughts, feelings, questions, notions, and misunderstandings that families face when trying to make sense of this problem. Interestingly enough, many of these same issues are common to both patients and loved ones.

Collusion Through Silence: Affected families often feel that they are in some way colluding with the patient, or they may actually collude. Collusion may be accomplished through silence or through ignoring or downplaying the seriousness of the behavior in the hope that perhaps it will disappear by itself. Such feelings of collusion may even degenerate into severe feelings of guilt.

Anger: Many patients have told me that when their families eventually discovered their behavior, usually through their apprehension, they were bombarded with outraged and angry denunciations—which may be perfectly understandable. A kleptomaniac's loved ones may be mentioned in the local newspaper, or they may be brought to the local police station. These families experience humiliation and shame and, not surprisingly, they often want to retaliate or in some way revenge themselves on the offending family member.

Frustration and Bewilderment: Despite even their best intentions, families of kleptomaniacs generally find themselves ill-equipped to deal with the complicated clinical and emotional aspects of the situation. They experience bewilderment, as they cannot for the life of them understand how, for instance, their son or daughter—in their eyes perhaps a good, even religious person—could so easily and willfully violate the rules and regulations of society. Their preaching, lecturing, and scolding has little, if any, effect on the stealing behavior. Finally, their tolerance for frustration diminishes. They give up hope and are left feeling impotent and powerless. They may even disown the person.

Denial: This is a fairly common reaction experienced by family members who are often trying their best to cope with a frustrating and demanding situation. Denial is a defense we all employ on occasion, especially when faced with a bitter or extremely demanding situation. Closing one's eyes to the piles of unexplained goods in the house is easier than imagining that a loved one is a thief.

Sadness and Despair: Like the kleptomaniacs themselves, family members voice hopelessness and depression when discussing the "shameful" behavior of a loved one. Their attempts at intervention do not appear to be working, and they remain unable to assuage the despair, depression, and ongoing anxiety of their parent, sibling, or child.

Aloneness: Perhaps the effect most keenly experienced by families, but the one most easily remedied, is the feeling of being the only person in the world who has a child or relative who steals for no apparent good reason. Kleptomaniacs often feel this way, too. Parents of a son or daughter suffering from kleptomania, for example, do not know where to turn and feel hesitant to share their secret with anyone. The feelings associated with revelation, as in the case of kleptomania, appear too overwhelmingly embarrassing to discuss with a friend or neighbor.

Trust: Families often have difficulty trusting their loved ones—feeling that if they are thieves, then they are liars and criminals as well. Families lose confidence in their relatives, may belittle them, and may even ask them to leave the house.

Guilt: For the families, guilt is often the final common denominator of all their collective feelings. Families may feel guilty about any number of issues, one of the more common being a sense that they are in some way responsible for this bizarre behavior. As families may be experiencing a variety of other feelings such as animosity or anger, another form of guilt may occur when they conclude that their jumbled emotional response to their loved one is unjust, wrong, or immoral. In this respect, perhaps the worst thing we can do is assume that great differences exist between those with mental illness or emotional impairment and ourselves.

CHAPTER 5

Roadblocks to Accuracy

"Yet I lusted to thieve and did it compelled by no hunger, no poverty."

— St. Augustine, 370 A.D.

The reasons for kleptomania's reportedly low prevalence rates are complex and varied. We cannot simply count those cases we know about—those apprehended, for example. Most kleptomaniacs are never apprehended and, like sufferers of eating disorders, do not come forward for treatment. How difficult is it to detect or count kleptomania sufferers?

While studying the reported cases of people suffering from kleptomania, I discovered, unlike people with mental illnesses or other emotional disorders, eighty-five percent of kleptomaniacs came to the attention of a mental health professional only *after* they had been referred by way of the court system. Unless they are apprehended, most kleptomaniacs will not come forward voluntarily. Because most who steal *don't* get caught, the vast majority of kleptomaniacs may not come to the attention of mental health professionals and, therefore, will be underrepresented in prevalence statistics.

Personal experience has shown that people harboring the secret of kleptomania and who seek treatment will almost never come to a mental health professional requesting help for *that* malady. They will invariably ask for help with *other* symptoms such as depression or anxiety.

What role do mental health professionals play in fostering statistical inaccuracies? As we have seen, some psychiatrists liken the stealing behavior seen in kleptomania to antisocial behavior, while others do not believe in the diagnosis at all. The truth is that the drive to steal appears to be no more "antisocial" than an anorexic's need to lie to her physician about how much food she is eating. By characterizing the theft as a purely antisocial act, kleptomania's legitimacy as a psychiatric disorder is compromised. Such characterizations dilute the statistical "pool" of those suffering from kleptomania, making the disorder appear to be less common.

Is kleptomania merely an invention? To the person suffering from the disorder, it certainly doesn't seem to be. A poem by Beth, illustrating both her despair and need for intervention, should serve as a reminder that, just because something is not visible, does not mean that it does not exist:

Hiding Places

What if
I tell you my name
And all my secrets?

Will you say them aloud there and then
So that they sear my hearing,
Or do them violence
Before you hand them back
Twisted as scrap and grey?
Will you linger over my secrets,
Let them grow like summer trees
A thousand arms into the sky
In directions I have not been taught
And color all before me and
Teach me ways to take?
If I offer all my secrets
Will you make them part of your mind
And give them light, show me
What I hide even from myself,
Caress my name and call me by it,
Draw me to yourself and give me Life?

Another reason for kleptomania's relative obscurity lies with several studies that revealed no cases of kleptomania in rather large pools of arrested or convicted shoplifters. However, the results of these studies are balanced by numerous others that reveal a prevalence of the disorder. It is possible that definitional difficulties inherent in diagnosing kleptomania came into play.

Perhaps the most important reason for reports of kleptomania's supposed rarity is that clinicians often do not have the skill or patience to detect the disorder. Doctors rarely ask patients about secretive disorders and do not wait long enough (or, in this climate of managed care, are not allowed sufficient time) for them to be revealed.

Kleptomania

PREVALENCE

Now that we have seen ways in which kleptomania has been underreported, let us examine some compelling reasons for its existence. Virtually all of the known data on kleptomania comes from *arrested* shoplifters, making it almost impossible to examine the population that steals but *doesn't* get arrested. According to available literature about this disorder, a large percentage of people steal, yet very few are apprehended. This is compounded by the fact that many of those people who witness stealing behaviors generally do not report it. It is for these reasons that we are unable to study the vast majority of people who steal.

Further diluting the pool of people who are kleptomaniacs and can be studied is the speculation that prominent people who are caught stealing often avoid arrest due to their social standing. Thus, shoplifters in general—and, perhaps, those exhibiting behaviors suggesting kleptomania—may escape our detection. Given all this information, how common is kleptomania? The bad news is that because known statistics on kleptomania are given as a percentage of apprehended shoplifters, a prevalence statistic for the general population is unknown. The good news is that we can make some estimates.

One rough method of predicting the prevalence of kleptomania is to isolate a group of individuals who suffer from several maladies, one of which is kleptomania. By knowing the prevalence of these people, we can estimate the prevalence of kleptomania. Some clinicians suggest that patients with eating disorders often suffer from kleptomania. Based on the prevalence of kleptomania in a given population of patients with eating disorders, and, knowing what the prevalence of eating disorders is, we can estimate that six out of every one thousand people may suffer from kleptomania.

Of course, there are many statistical problems with estimating prevalence rates using this technique. These numbers are only preliminary and need to be confirmed (or refuted or revised) by further experimental techniques. If it can be shown, however, that kleptomania is as common (or even half as common) as these preliminary statistics indicate, this disorder would be found more frequently than many mental illnesses and disorders.

What else can we know about the demographics of kleptomania? Although once again these are only preliminary, adding the number of cases in my own practice to those I have surveyed in diagnostic literature, the average age of a klepto-maniac at the time of evaluation or diagnosis, is 35+12.6 for women (range, 17-57) and 50+16.1 for men (range, 25-68). The average age for both sexes at the time of psychiatric evaluation is 38+14.3. The average age of onset is 20+12.5 for women (range 6-44). There is not enough data to speculate about the average age of onset in men.

KLEPTOMANIA FACTS

• The term "kleptomania" was introduced in 1838. It comes from the Greek for "stealing insanity."
• It has been said that as many as 6 in every 1000 people are afflicted with kleptomania.
• Women constitute between 77% and 81% of all reported cases of kleptomania.
• Business losses from theft, some of which are due to kleptomania, vary. The *Grand Rapids Press* reported $9

billion in losses in 1996, the *Boston Globe* reported $24 billion in losses in 1993, the *Detroit Free Press* reported $35 billion in losses in 1992 and other reports range from $8 billion to $50 billion in losses annually.

• Of the $9.7 billion that shoplifting costs retailers and consumers annually, an estimated $485 million is credited to kleptomaniacs.

• Approximately 2 million Americans a year are charged with shoplifting. It is estimated that for every arrest another thirty-five people get away with their spoils.

• Many people with kleptomania hide their secret, preferring to restrict shopping activity rather than seek professional care. For this reason, the exact number of people suffering from kleptomania is unknown, but estimates are probably much lower than the real numbers.

• The average age of female patients at the time of evaluation is thirty-five-years-old and for male patients it jumps to fifty-years-old.

• The average age of a patient at the onset of the disorder for women is twenty-years-old and for men it is unknown.

According to statistics, the typically lengthy time period between onset of stealing behaviors and diagnosis seems to support the proposition that kleptomania is an episodic behavior that is extremely difficult to self-extinguish and difficult to detect. It also lends credence to the observation that kleptomaniacs carry the burden of their secret alone. The traditional belief that kleptomania first develops in a middle-aged woman in response to an acute loss, such as a child's leaving home, seems incongruous. Rather, it seems clear that the disorder represents a pattern established early on in life.

Available data implies that the vast majority of people suffering from kleptomania are married—although this does not imply that the marriages are necessarily happy ones.

Information regarding social class, rural and urban distribution, race, or religion is sketchy. Literary researchers, Schlueter, et. al., found that "nonrational" shoplifters (kleptomaniacs) were more likely to be of faiths other than Catholic or Protestant, and were better educated. These researchers also found no difference in race between the "nonrational" and ordinary thieves. It is not known whether this data is reliable.

There are likely huge numbers of kleptomaniacs about whom we know nothing. Most have never been arrested, have not come to our attention, and, most likely, have either never entered treatment or, if they have, have not revealed this secret to their therapists. However, my own clinical experience indicates that when kleptomania sufferers discover that others are experiencing the same behaviors they are, it becomes easier for them to begin to discuss similar personal areas of their own lives.

CHAPTER 6

The Gender Question: Whose Problem is This Anyway?

"For years I would take things from family members and then return them."

– Mike

Whether accurate or not, kleptomania has long been considered to be an almost exclusive disorder of women. While there have been numerous reports of kleptomania in men (and we will look at a few), such cases are often "contaminated" by other signs and symptoms that leave the diagnosis in question.

We have already discussed the caricature of a kleptomaniac—a bent-over, orgasmic, middle-aged woman slinking around stores with a shopping cart. While offering much in the way of theory and understanding, we have seen how some mental health practitioners have added to the maze of misunderstanding and misrepresentation. Is kleptomania a problem for men, for women, or for both sexes?

POLITICALLY CORRECT: CAN WE EVER KNOW?

For a variety of reasons, it is becoming increasingly difficult to discuss the relative roles of the sexes in various mental illnesses or disorders. In fact, gender has become a particularly difficult topic to discuss openly. Why? For many, discussing the roles of the sexes in mental disorders is tantamount to blaming the victim. Those that would criticize theoreticians, however, fail to recognize the difference between being judgmental and simply observing and pointing out factual data.

Have some researchers acted with insensitivity? Absolutely. Some early psychoanalytic writers, although otherwise skilled at uncovering important unconscious mechanisms, were sometimes equally skilled at belittling women in one way or another. It was not long ago, for example, that psychiatric as well as nonpsychiatric physicians were attributing many ailments, including kleptomania, solely to dysfunctions of the female reproductive system. Of course, repudiation of important ideas or factual findings or their replacement with inaccurate or even ridiculous theories undermines and damages psychiatry's reputation. As we discuss gender, we will try to do so in a way that should feel comfortable to most.

WOMEN & MEN: CASES, LITERATURE, AND CLINICAL OBSERVATIONS

From the earliest journal entries to more recent studies, most researchers have found that women constitute the vast majority of those diagnosed with kleptomania. Some researchers feel that kleptomania is an invention forced upon women by male physicians during the Victorian era, when shopping in department stores became fashionable. This theory held that women became tempted to steal because stores displayed their goods within physical reach. Since most consumers were women, they were the willing victims, seduced to take by sheer desire and convenience. This theory further poses that male physicians, in order to maintain their dominance, victimized women by classifying them as mentally ill, thus creating a new generation of weak, victimized, mentally ill, powerless women.

Unfortunately, these theories do a disservice to women by insisting that "kleptomania" exists only as a male fantasy. It appears unlikely that kleptomania resulted from or appeared for the first time during the Victorian era. There are numerous documented cases of the types of behaviors seen in kleptomania as early as 1799. Since it is highly probable that virtually every human behavior that exists now existed years ago, it stands to reason that kleptomania is nothing new.

Recently, Louise Kaplan, in her scholarly book, *Female Perversions*, accepts the notion that the majority of kleptomaniacs are women. Historically, kleptomania was so curious a phenomenon that accounts of such behavior in women could be seen in virtually every form of media imaginable today. In 1799, for example, novelist Jane Austen's aunt, a wealthy woman with no criminal record, was apprehended for stealing a card of lace. The theft was so uncharacteristic for someone of her social position that the storekeeper, who had accused her of the theft, had *his* character attacked in court. In the early 1800's, Benjamin Rush, an early psychiatrist, noted the case of an upstanding woman who "when she could lay her hands on nothing more valuable, she would often at the table of a friend fill her pockets secretly with bread."

My own experience in both private and hospital-based practice seems to parallel the traditional portrayal of kleptomania as a disorder of women. In fact, when I carefully studied case literature approximating the criteria for klepto-mania, 80 percent turned out to be women. Given this, is it true that most kleptomaniacs are women? Not necessarily. Women are more likely than men to refer themselves for psy-chiatric help. My research revealed that, although it is rare for a kleptomaniac to seek treatment for that particular condition, the few who did come voluntarily for psychiatric assessment were women.

Another confounding fact is that the courts may be more inclined to send male shoplifters (some of whom may be kleptomaniacs) to prison, while women shoplifters tradition-ally end up in psychiatric treatment. For example, Medlicott describes the case of a man who was *incarcerated for fourteen years* for the repetitive theft of trucks and bicycles that he *abandoned shortly after taking them*!

BAD, MAD, OR SAD?

Is it possible that kleptomania is equally prevalent in both sexes? Do men go to jail rather than a hospital when they steal without obvious reason? Do women become "sad" (depressed) or even "mad" (insane) when unduly stressed? When men are stressed or distressed, do they become "bad" or violent? Are there male kleptomaniacs tucked away in prisons?

One way to explore the possible existence of "male" kleptomania would be to screen for kleptomania in a male penal setting. While we may see behaviors consistent with kleptomania, however, we will likely also detect a variety of their clinical and non-clinical baggage—antisocial signs and symptoms. A diagnosis of kleptomania would be very difficult, if not impossible. Additionally, as we will see in some of the following examples, the reliability or truthfulness of inmates can be poor.

Mike: When I first met Mike, a twenty-three-year-old man, he was awaiting trial on charges of armed robbery. Mike had been transferred to the prison hospital after exhibiting extreme despair, anxiety, and severe depression. He had been found hanging in his cell, but was quickly cut down.

In the interview, Mike described a very tumultuous childhood. His father, who was extremely abusive, had raped Mike's mother and sisters repeatedly and had once hung Mike upside down out of the window for taking too much food for dinner. While Mike denied the types of behavior ordinarily attributed to antisocial people—setting fires, abuse of animals, truancy, or running away from home—he had a history of repeated arrests for crimes such as rape, robbery, and assaults.

Mike was friendly, cooperative, and without psychosis. Indeed, no delusions or hallucinations were present. Mike stated that he had a serious drug and alcohol problem and had been treated for depression in a psychiatric hospital many years prior to his incarceration. He was anxious to be discharged from the prison hospital so that he could return to his prison unit.

Quite spontaneously, Mike also told me that he was a "kleptomaniac." Noting Mike's history of theft, I assumed he was referring to his theft charges. However, he told me that for years, particularly at home, he would often take objects from family members and then return them a short time later. He had stolen a ring from his mother and money from his father. When he was twenty, he stole a toy doll from his younger brother's crib. All the items were returned shortly after he had taken them.

As we will see later, many of Mike's early life experiences are not necessarily inconsistent with the experiences of those suffering from kleptomania. However, Mike's other associated symptoms—antisocial behavior, violence, and drug use—clearly are not. While a diagnosis of antisocial personality and kleptomania are technically inconsistent with each other, if the intensity of Mike's drive to steal items that he quickly returned is genuine, it would be theoretically possible to assume that the prisons may be holding male kleptomaniacs. On the other hand, such cases are so mired with antisocial characteristics that we may never be able to get at the truth.

George: George was a thirty-five-year-old man who had been referred to me by his probation officer. He had been accused of making harassing phone calls to a woman he claimed he did not know. He was a difficult person to assess (because of his guarded and uncooperative nature). An extremely obese man and poorly groomed, he was physically intimidating. During the interview he was hostile, withholding, and irritable. He spoke only when questioned and answered in curt bursts of extreme emotion.

George told me that he only made obscene phone calls when drunk, and that he had not made any in seven months. As a child, George said he had been truant and had started to use alcohol at an early age. He refused to discuss the details of his childhood with me.

He had been arrested on numerous occasions for a variety of infractions, including being drunk and disorderly and making obscene calls, and had served time in prison. He didn't elicit a great deal of sympathy.

Upon further questioning, he also acknowledged being arrested on three other occasions. When pressed, with great hesitation, George told me that his other arrests were for shoplifting. These offenses seemed out of character for him; his other crimes bordered on being potentially violent or menacing. Furthermore, while George was morbidly obese and obviously did not take very good care of himself, he chose to steal *vitamins,* for reasons he could not explain.

Sam: Sam, a twenty-two-year-old homosexual, was admitted to a local psychiatric hospital after he had stabbed himself. While in the unit, he allegedly stole some flowers from another patient's room and was asked to leave the hospital. He was then readmitted to another facility with complaints of suicidal ideation. At his interview, he appeared eccentric with a bizarre haircut. He openly admitted his homosexuality and stated that he had recently had a fight with his lover. He had also recently been diagnosed as HIV-positive.

Sam admitted having at least five prior psychiatric admissions for suicidal ideation and gestures. His first contact with mental health care had occurred at fourteen, when he developed gender identity issues and exhibited truancy problems. Upon further questioning, Sam admitted that he had "no childhood." His father had died when he was a child, and he was given responsibility to run the home.

Sam acknowledged a severe history of sexual abuse that began at age five. He was repeatedly sexually assaulted by his father, brother, uncle, and, later, his stepfather. Sam's stepfather would become so intoxicated that, according to Sam, "My stepfather would mistake me for my mother."

At age fourteen, after the sexual abuse ceased, Sam began to use heavy drugs, including cocaine, heroin, and alcohol. Sam's legal history began with breaking and entering. He was currently awaiting trial on a variety of other charges. When confronted with his behavior, he cautiously admitted stealing on numerous occasions. He stated that it began on a dare to steal a candy bar. Sam said that stealing helped to reduce his anxiety, and that he often had no memory of the act. In the psychiatric unit, he was provoking and noncompliant. He was caught stealing at times when it made little sense. Furthermore, he did not seem overly concerned with concealing his behavior.

The difficult nature of these men, coupled with their criminal histories and self-defeating and often violent behaviors, clearly complicates their clinical pictures. Their stories elicited little sympathy from those around them. Their behaviors were viewed as strictly criminal. While the men were quite bold in their willingness to discuss their criminal pasts, they were extremely guarded when asked to discuss their thievery. Interestingly, this unwillingness to disclose the details of an important habit is not dissimilar to that found in women who steal.

DOING VS. FEELING

Despite the fact that male kleptomania does exist, the hypothesis that women constitute the majority of those suffering from kleptomania appears true. Dr. Samuel Guze, a well-respected psychiatrist, has done a great deal of research in the area of gender, criminality, and mental illness. His studies have led to some instructive conclusions.

Guze looked at a variety of people who had committed felony offenses. In exploring the differences between the sexes, he noticed that, given the same difficult developmental environments in childhood, males and females who grew up to be felons reflected different psychiatric diagnoses. Males became more overtly antisocial, while females developed signs and symptoms more consistent with what was once called "hysteria"—becoming, among other things, depressed, anxious, and moody. These findings do not mean that kleptomaniacs are hysterical. However, it could mean that, given the same difficult childhood, men and women with difficulty in controlling their impulses may express this in different ways. Men may "do" (the crime and time) while women in the majority may "feel" (depression and anxiety).

Overtly aggressive behaviors such as pyromania, pathological gambling, and intermittent explosive disorders predominate in men, while women tend to engage in seemingly less physically destructive behaviors.

However, although kleptomania appears more common in women, it remains an important issue for everyone.

CHAPTER 7

Kleptomania and Criminality

"I know it's wrong, but I do it anyway!"

– Paula, a patient

Given the unusual nature of the signs and symptoms of those suffering from kleptomania, one must ask why these people put themselves at risk simply to take things that do not belong to them and which they don't need? Kleptomaniacs run the distinct risk of being considered criminals rather than patients. They are conscious of their illegal behavior, often feel remorse and guilt over it, and yet cannot stop it—a terrifying predicament.

In fact it is nearly impossible to discuss kleptomania without discussing sociopathy. Sociopathy (antisocial or psychopathic behavior or personality) denotes a pervasive style of interacting angrily with one's surroundings. Antisocial people may lie, cheat, be abusive toward others, and be notoriously untrustworthy. Some may even be violent. They are generally unreliable, express little—if any—genuine remorse for their wrongdoing, and are unable to experience the important quality of empathy. Prisons are full of these people.

If stealing is explained by a diagnosis of antisocial personality disorder, then kleptomania as a diagnostic possibility is excluded. Because antisocial people often steal, and kleptomania is a stealing disorder, kleptomaniacs are often characterized as criminals, regardless of diagnostic considerations. What is the relationship between kleptomania and antisocial personality disorder, if any? The perception that kleptomania is in some way related to sociopathy is likely rooted in four observations: 1) kleptomania is thievery; 2) most thieves go to jail; 3) kleptomaniacs may resist sincere efforts at treatment; and 4) kleptomaniacs may use the issue of "irresistibility" as an excuse to steal.

ANYWAY YOU SLICE IT, KLEPTOMANIA IS STEALING

While it might seem absurd to some, we cannot escape the truism that the kleptomaniac engages in an illegal activity, violates community standards, and causes personal and business losses. Even though it is difficult to understand, patients are acutely aware of these issues. Unlike the antisocial person, the kleptomaniac struggles with the notion of good and bad, right and wrong, and will often confess that "It makes me feel like a bad person. I don't associate my behavior with any disorder. I'm just a bad person. Bad people do this, so I must be bad. I am forever trying to convince my therapist that I don't have a conscience, and that I'm just a bad person."

Is the kleptomaniac merely an opportunistic criminal? Does the stealing carried out by kleptomaniacs suggest that the patient has an antisocial or sociopathic personality? Do patients have other characteristics and qualities consistent with sociopathy? Is the stealing behavior the sole aggressive trait in an otherwise honest person?

Kleptomania's place in the spectrum of mental disorders is unique and unclear. Unlike schizophrenia or manic-depressive illness, kleptomania is not a *major* mental illness. As we will see, kleptomaniacs have little in common with the criminal mind. Kleptomania's relationship to criminality is, however, one of its most interesting and poorly understood features. By its very nature, kleptomania appears to fall somewhere between criminality (because of the theft) and mental illness (because of the bizarre nature of the act). Few emotionally disordered people carry with them the dubious distinction of being both perpetrator and victim, as is the case with kleptomania. History affords some reasons for this duality.

KLEPTOMANIA AND SOCIOPATHY: A HISTORICAL PERSPECTIVE

Why have certain mental health professionals viewed kleptomania in the past with great suspicion? Diagnosing a mental disorder to explain an illegal act might have appeared to be an excuse for the behavior—perhaps even seeming to discourage patients from taking responsibility for themselves. Some psychiatrists in the past classified kleptomania as a "psychopathic" (or sociopathic) disorder, often considering it to be little more than common criminality. Patients exhibited little genuine guilt or remorse over their acts of thievery or possessed a personality structure akin to those seen with antisocial characters.

Other psychiatrists, however, were struck by the specific nature of the illegal act and the fact that, outwardly, the person appeared to be an otherwise honest, "upstanding citizen." As early as the beginning of the nineteenth century, psychiatrist Benjamin Rush, describing what would eventually be termed kleptomania, recognized the apparently limited role that the antisocial act of stealing played in a person's makeup:

"There are persons who are moved to the highest degree as to certain duties, but who, nonetheless, live under the influence of some one vice. In one instance, a woman was exemplary in her obedience to every command of the moral law except one—she could not refrain from stealing. What made this vice more remarkable was that she was in easy circumstances and not addicted to extravagances in any thing ... She both confessed and lamented her crime."

Dr. Rush went on to point out that, were it not for the one "moral failure" of the patient—stealing—she would be a quite ordinary, honest citizen. His patient freely admitted her behavior and expressed remorse.

In later years, while discussing the development of kleptomania in their patients, psychoanalysts had many different theories and ideas related to the seemingly antisocial behavior typical of this disorder. Theorizing that kleptomaniacs actually steal because they unconsciously want to be apprehended and punished, some psychiatrists attributed the stealing behavior to the person's punitive conscience. Others, however, felt that kleptomaniacs actually had a lack of conscience and were driven to steal for more purely antisocial and self-serving reasons.

TREATMENT REFUSAL VS. SOCIOPATHY

Kleptomaniacs are notoriously difficult to treat. They often refuse to participate or fail to appear for appointments. It is quite common for those suffering from kleptomania to express ambivalence about receiving treatment. They may be labeled as sociopathic because of their apparent unwillingness to forfeit the risky stealing behavior by submitting to treatment. For example, a clinical vignette from Dr. Wittels' writings states:

> *"Such 'patients' come for treatment not because they wish to change but because they have been threatened by the law. Then they are eager to get an attestation that they are ill and ask the judge to postpone prosecution for the sake of treatment. In their predicaments they can describe quite dramatically how badly off they are 'imprisoned all night with drunkards, prostitutes and all kinds of bums. . . I, a lady, . . . my family disgraced. . . Save me, doctor. . . I know you can cure me.' As soon as we have succeeded in persuading the judge of the pathological nature of the situation, the patient's demeanor changes: 'What, after all, is it that you wish to cure, doctor? I am not sick. I was a thief, I grant you, but I promise that I will never do such a thing again.' . . . Actually, however, our little lady will repeat the performance. . ."*

In describing the case of a sixteen-year-old female who had been caught stealing and hoarding goods while residing at a girls' school, Dr. Wittels reports what happened during several therapy sessions. When asked why she had committed these thefts, she shrugs her shoulders and says that she does not know:

> *"Do you really want to get rid of this trouble?"*
> *"Of course," replies the girl.*
> *"Isn't it distressing for a young girl of such good family, attractive and well brought up, to jeopardize her future by such foolish behavior?"*
> *"Distressing indeed," replies the girl.*

However, Wittels writes that the girl misses her first appointment and he decides that she is not serious about the matter. When the girl calls a week later to ask if she can come in again, Wittels tells her that he can not do anything to help her if she does not want his help and that he needs her total cooperation to accomplish results.

The girl assures Wittels that she is indeed sincere in her desire to be helped with her "terrible habit." Although Wittels finds her to be outwardly serene and of good will, he finds that despite her assurances, the girl's actions reveal her true position on the matter. He writes that, "Sometimes she comes to her appointments and sometimes she doesn't. The excuses become more and more threadbare and, finally, the treatment has to be stopped."

However, those who label kleptomania sufferers in this manner may be interpreting the incredible drive to steal and accompanying treatment ambivalence as a lack of remorse or guilt. This misconception would most certainly help confirm the "sociopathic" hypothesis. However, the interpretation is very likely inaccurate. For the person suffering from kleptomania, the intense drive to steal and keep stealing may be no more antisocial than the anorexic's need to lie to her family or physician about the quality and quantity of her daily food intake.

THE PROBLEM OF IRRESISTIBILITY

Perhaps no other feature of any emotional disorder is ultimately more destructive and regressive than the notion of "irresistibility." Irresistibility implies that something is out of someone's control, or that they do not possess the ability to resist an impulse. The concept of irresistibility seems to remove responsibility from the person and instead attributes maladaptive behavior to some unseen inner demon. Many sufferers tell me themselves that the impulses are irresistible—despite the fact that they frequently avoid capture by not stealing when being directly observed and have the ability to stay away from stores to prevent themselves from committing the acts.

Is kleptomania truly irresistible? If so, how irresistible? Is it analogous to a drug or cigarette habit? Why can most patients avoid stealing by staying away from shops? If, for some reason, we find it not entirely irresistible, does the behavior then cease to be kleptomania and become something else? Why can most kleptomaniacs resist the temptation to steal if they are under direct observation?

One theory is that, initially, stealing may start out as an option. As the kleptomaniac reaps the benefits of taking, the urge may then become somewhat more difficult to ignore. Stealing certainly *seems* or *feels* irresistible (or at least necessary), but it very likely is not—at least not all the time. As we learn more about kleptomania, perhaps some of these questions and issues will have suitable explanations. Later, we'll take a look at some possible biological theories that could account for the "addictive-like" quality of kleptomania.

KLEPTOMANIA'S RELATIONSHIP TO SOCIOPATHY

Theories that lump kleptomania together with antisocial diagnoses are likely to be far too simplistic. Such theories also fail to take into account the kinds of symptoms present in antisocial individuals—but not present in kleptomania. In my experience, both in reviewing the literature and in my own practice, it seems inaccurate to classify those with the disorder as criminals or otherwise antisocial. Study after study reveals that, for the most part, people suffering from kleptomania do not have the kind of character traits present in sociopathic individuals. When discussing their behavior, the majority of individuals are genuinely remorseful and guilt-ridden. It is typical for them to say "I feel guilty every time someone steals something. Somehow, I feel like I infected them with myself. It reminds me of what I've done. I feel horrible, yet I do it again!"

One deeply religious patient I treated became so distraught that she wept with shame when discussing her stealing behavior and its relation to immorality. "I know it's wrong, but I do it anyway!" she cried.

Data indicate that, while the act itself (taken in isolation and by its very nature) may be sociopathic, the personality structure is not. There are no data, for example, that characterize kleptomaniacs as violent, truant, involved in physical fights, using weapons, or destroying personal property. Also, kleptomaniacs do not brag about their conquests. What adds to the controversy is that patients can and do exhibit sorrow and remorse over their actions, but continue to steal anyway. This does not indicate sociopathy. The objective is not material gain and financial profit—it is the very act of stealing.

Remember, there is no "pure" anything in mental health diagnoses. I have had patients tell me that they feel terribly guilty about their behavior and, at the same time, often feel entitled to take what does not belong to them. Can kleptomania and sociopathy be at all related? There are, of course, exceptions. Just as most people have a mild smattering of sociopathic traits, so, too, can the patient suffering from kleptomania. Just as the psychotic or depressed person may share many different characteristics wholly unrelated to their primary diagnosis, the kleptomaniac may show a variety of signs and symptoms unrelated to kleptomania itself.

One thing is certain: the drive to steal appears to be quite intense—so much so that, even though they can afford to buy the goods, kleptomaniacs are willing to risk arrest in order to steal things they do not need. If the stealing act in kleptomania does not imply a sociopathic core, then what are its possible functions? What is at the root? One suggestion may be that, while people who steal for ordinary material gain exhibit far more antisocial tendencies, those suffering from kleptomania and other kinds of nonsensical stealing tend to be depressed, anxious, and isolated. The overwhelming majority of psychiatric literature on kleptomania focuses on the issues of depression and anxiety. What is the relationship between theft and depression? In the following chapter, we will explore the unique partnership between depression, anxiety, and stealing.

CHAPTER 8

Kleptomania's Hallmarks: Depression and Anxiety

I've been getting nervous. If I take a chair into the closet (to see 200 stolen dresses) *and close the door, it calms me down."*
— A Russian Immigrant

There are often significant differences between sufferers of kleptomania, but what about commonalities? If they exist, might this clinical information help us understand or further unravel the mysteries of kleptomania? Susan's life was characterized by persistent depression, social isolation, and anxiety. Her childhood was punctuated by traumatic experiences, and she struggled to feel comfortable with other people. Although working, she found interacting with her peers painful and intimidating. Is Susan alone? Are her problems unique?

Jane, thirty-three-year-old lawyer, complained of perpetual sadness and anxiety. She had been taking numerous antidepressant medications, but nothing seemed to help. In addition to her stealing behavior, she experienced chronic addition to her stealing behavior, she experienced chronic suicidal feelings and, when stressed, threatened to jump in front of a car.

Frieda, a prim, forty-two-year-old deeply religious woman, had battled depression and kleptomania for much of her life. Her depression was so extensive and severe that she had never been able to hold a job. Frieda had been hospitalized for depression and suicidal thoughts over one hundred times. Despite attempts to treat her depression with medication, nothing seemed to help.

Another patient, Carol, expressed the sad realities of persistent, devastating anxiety in this way:

> *"I also have a terrible anxiety problem. I worry all the time. I worry that the house will catch on fire, or carbon monoxide will get us. I'm fearful that people do not like me, and I get anxious when someone watches me. I can't relax."*

Any similarities? While every patient has his or her own particular personality style, traits, and characteristics, the majority of kleptomaniacs struggle with feelings of depression or anxiety, the common clinical threads. Unable to pull themselves out, some become entrenched in sadness and are unable to enjoy life. Feeling as though they are about to take an examination for which they have not studied, they become immobilized by fear and anxiety. Some even attempt suicide.

Depression and anxiety, the common threads that link one sufferer to another, are the hallmarks of kleptomania. How bad is it?

For Susan, depression and anxiety meant an impoverished social life. For others, debilitating depression and anxiety were harbingers of suicidal feelings and gestures. Affecting both work and play, depression and anxiety are notorious for depleting energy. Pleasure, self-confidence, and a strong sense of identity are all drained. What is the relationship between depression, anxiety, and kleptomania? Does a history of chronic or episodic sadness or anxiety increase the risk of developing kleptomania? Let us take a look at some theoretical and historical perspectives on the origins of kleptomania and its relationship to depression and anxiety.

DEPRESSION AND ANXIETY

Today, the label "depression" has become common. But what is it? As with anything else in psychiatry, depression means different things to different people. On occasion, everyone feels blue or sad. With time or a little help from supportive loved ones, most of us manage to lift ourselves from this temporary state and move on. However, for many people depression can be a far worse experience. Clinically, depression is a state of sadness that can be of varying degrees. Some depressions are severe: patients may not be able to get out of bed, take care of their personal hygiene, or speak. Those with severe depression may become psychotic and hear voices or experience delusions. In milder forms sufferers may feel fatigued, lack energy, and experience diminished sexual interest or pleasure in typically pleasurable things. They may also complain of too much or too little sleep and may have a disturbed appetite. Loss of self-esteem, poor concentration, chronic irritability, mood swings, and suicidal feelings may be present. Depression can be an episodic response to a real or perceived loss, or it may be ongoing. Depression can be "endogenous"—created from within and seemingly unrelated to any identifiable problem.

What is anxiety? Its definition, like that of depression, can vary. Anxiety can encompass a wide array of possible signs and symptoms: worry, sweating, feeling "keyed up," feeling nervous, apprehension, or becoming easily startled. Anxiety generally appears when some sort of danger, either conscious or unconscious, is present. In Susan's case, she often became anxious when discussing issues of intimacy. In its most severe form, anxiety can be devastating, leading to immobility and despair.

For over one hundred years, researchers have recognized that depression and anxiety are frequently observed in patients suffering from kleptomania. In both my referenced and personal cases, the vast majority of kleptomaniacs have strong personal and family histories of both depression and anxiety. While most researchers agree that depression and anxiety play an important role in the life of the kleptomaniac, there is less agreement on more specific questions. How severe is the depression? How intense are the anxiety states? How long have they been present? Are the symptoms permanent, or do they come and go?

Evidence suggests that there is no absolute or fixed degree of severity. The kinds of depression found in kleptomaniacs vary considerably. Susan's depression allowed her to function at work but severely restricted her ability to enjoy herself socially. While most people are able to function without psychiatric hospitalization, the majority of kleptomaniacs seem to suffer from varying degrees of lifelong depression or anxiety. Most are able to work, and many feel comfortable interacting socially. But many have poor self-esteem and suffer from poor self-images and diminished self-worth. On the other hand, a minority are significantly impaired. They are often hospitalized for depression, anxiety, or suicidal urges.

Regardless of the specific types of depression, the evidence is overwhelming that not only do patients have extensive histories of depression, but they may actually experience an acute exacerbation of depression or anxiety immediately prior to stealing. Both depression and anxiety are often precursors to many kinds of theft.

THE ROOTS OF KLEPTOMANIA

Past researchers have sought to explain the relationship between depression, anxiety, and the origins of kleptomania. Their theories range from the gynecological explanations which were popular in the 1800's to present biological pathways. The bulk of research was done in the first part of the twentieth century. During this era, through lengthy analysis of troubled patients, numerous classically trained psychoanalysts worked towards a comprehensive understanding of kleptomania. Most felt that depression, anxiety, and kleptomania were likely the end result of some greater primary pathology.

In fact, some psychiatrists suggested that stealing was a symptom of an underlying conflict: the act of stealing unneeded objects was a symbolic representation of an unconscious attempt to fix an unresolved emotional problem. The theft of unneeded objects was generally seen as an attempt to gratify id impulses, an expression of infantile needs, a form of restitution, and a symbolic punishment directed toward those who failed to provide love.

This rather long-winded explanation implies that, for

those who had suffered in some way during infancy or child-hood, stealing was a symbolic attempt to make up for early deprivations and represented an attempt to symbolically "get back" at those who did the depriving.

Another theory held that, since most kleptomaniacs were women, the items stolen symbolically represented their attempts to obtain a penis.

What about the actual object stolen? Might it clue us in to a sufferer's pathology? While many psychiatrists empha-sized the symbolic nature of the act of stealing, some saw meaning in the stolen object itself. Only recently, in a maga-zine article written by Yagoda, Cupchik described what hap-pened to a Russian immigrant "who was arrested after stealing three dresses from a fashionable department store. Noting her erratic behavior, the police went to her house, where they found 200 dresses in a walk-in closet, their price tags still on. She told the police, 'I've been getting nervous. If I take a chair into the closet and close the door, it calms me down.'"

Cupchik revealed that the woman's father had died in her arms while she was still a child. Her mother, a dress-maker, was ill and unable to work. As a girl, the patient was forced to trade her own dresses to wealthy women for food. Several weeks prior to her arrest, her pet dog had to be put to sleep; this trauma, the author concluded, reawakened her shame, humiliation, and repression. Stealing made her feel whole again.

While this case might better be explained as patho-logical grief or bereavement, it serves to demonstrate the scope of theft and its possible symbolic value. However, most cases do not appear to be that easily explained.

While the debate rages on, some case reports empha-size the importance of the act of stealing rather than those that highlight the importance of the stolen goods themselves. Psychoanalyst Michael Beldoch, M.D., discussing the analysis of a patient and her actions, writes in a letter:

> *"She reported in an analytic hour that she had seen my coat in the coat closet, had rubbed her cheek over the sleeve, and had had an intense desire to steal the coat. When I asked her what would happen if I gave her the coat, she told me that it would be useless to her; only if it still belonged to me could she steal it and thus have (something of) me."*

The patient obviously derived benefit not from possessing the coat, but from the actual act of taking it. She likely would have taken anything belonging to the doctor.

Can we make any conclusive or definitive statements about kleptomania's origins? The theories seem to reach to all corners of the clinical globe. Is there a common denominator? In retrospect, some cases of stealing in kleptomania appear to be responses to early deprivations or losses. Symbolically, "stealing back" something once possessed and now lost was a historical theory—and still is. While these theories are interesting, and perhaps relevant since there is no clear data to suggest that such knowledge alone is helpful in alleviating patient symptoms, they are not necessarily helpful.

HOW DOES CRIME PAY?

What is the link between stealing, depression, and anxiety? We know that stealing brings tremendous, albeit temporary, relief of stress and anxiety. Patients suffering from kleptomania can experience relief of tension or both relief and pleasure from the act of stealing. Since the majority of kleptomaniacs suffer from depression, could the same "relief" system that benefits the anxious kleptomaniac serve also as an antidepressant?

Human beings typically do things to or for themselves when they do not feel well emotionally—take a vacation, purchase a new appliance, or take a day off from work. The act of stealing may represent an emotionally compromised person's attempt to relieve feelings of depression and self-loathing.

This is not a new idea. As early as 1911, Dr. Pierre Janet, a well-known psychiatrist, described the case of a woman who found relief from her depressive symptoms through the stimulation provided by shoplifting. In a more contemporary case, Dr. D.A. Fishbain described the case of a woman with a history of depression and kleptomania who masturbated while shoplifting. Fishbain felt that the patient's depression was a stimulus to risk-taking behavior which had an antidepressant effect.

Most of the information about kleptomania has been theoretical, not practical, and of limited use to sufferers. These cases are important because they emphasize the practical value of theft for the kleptomaniac.

Later, we will use this data to further study the physiological and emotional mechanisms present in the kleptomaniac's complex set of behaviors.

CHAPTER 9

Kleptomania: The Tip of the Diagnostic Iceberg?

"I have scars from cutting that run up my arms. I actually just burned myself last week."

– Paula

Thirty-two-year-old Jenny, slender and intense looking, is a woman with a lifelong history of stormy, impersonal relationships, depression, anxiety, bulimia, and suicidal feelings. Over the course of her life, she has engaged in repetitive self-mutilation and cutting. She has burned her increasingly scarred body at least twice every week. Despite her self-loathing, Jenny had been able to work as an assistant in a medical school laboratory, but, eventually stole some needles and injected herself with dirt. She seemed incapable of stopping herself from ingesting dozens of candy bars within a short period of time, yet she tried to lose weight by eating undercooked pork, hoping the meat would be infested with parasites. She abused alcohol and tried to kill herself dozens of times by overdosing. Several years ago, she was arrested for the theft of some magazines and chewing gum. She continued to steal several times a week and was even refused services by several therapists for stealing items from their offices.

Though Jenny's case represents an atypical and extreme example, it also raises a much debated question concerning kleptomania: Does kleptomania exist by itself, or is it connected to other, more severe disorders?

ONE OR MANY DISORDERS?

Let us return briefly to Susan. Susan did not come to therapy for help with the specific complaint of stealing. This revelation came years later. She suffered from a variety of other problems. For example, she found it difficult to interact well with others. In time, it was revealed that she had had a tumultuous childhood, as well as interpersonal difficulties. She also had problems with intimacy and mood swings, as well as symptoms of depression and anxiety.

Looking back, Susan's constellation of complaints raises some interesting questions. Is kleptomania a "monomania?" Is it the only malady in an otherwise healthy body? Does her case—and others like it—dispel the belief that kleptomania exists in isolation? Is kleptomania merely a symptom of some larger mental disorder?

Historically, many clinicians felt that kleptomania stood on its own, existing independently of any other problem. As such, it was seen as a separate, distinct diagnosis. The stealing behavior was considered to be the only "aberration" in an otherwise normal person (as in Dr. Rush's case of the woman who stole bread from her friend's dinner table, but who appeared to be of otherwise high "moral character").

The early belief that kleptomaniacs had only one exclusive problem (theft, for example) is illustrated in the case of Jane Austen's aunt, Mrs. Jane Leigh-Perrot. As we've seen, Mrs. Leigh-Perrot, a wealthy woman with no criminal record, was tried for the alleged theft of a card of lace. This theft was considered so uncharacteristic for someone of her position that she was acquitted and the character of the shop-keeper who had made the accusation was attacked in court.

A literary description of Mrs. Leigh-Perrot includes the fact that she was fifty-four, childless, quiet, and reserved. Her husband suffered from gout and may have been hypochondriacal, leaving her with little emotional support. As we will see later, these observations may have significance as we decide whether kleptomania exists in isolation.

As early researchers and psychiatrists continued their efforts to classify mental disorders, interesting new view-points developed. The concept of a class of disorders that would later include kleptomania emerged from Phillipe Pinel's classification work in the early nineteenth century. Although he did not discuss kleptomania specifically, Pinel classified as "moral insanities" those disorders considered to be "a morbid perversion of the natural feelings, affections, inclinations, temper, habits, moral disposition, and natural impulses."

E. Esquirol, a student of Pinel, later described these as deviant behaviors characterized by involuntary, instinctive, and irresistible actions. Monomania, or "one madness," implied that the person was otherwise completely normal but for the one deviant behavior. Along with Dr. Marc, Esquirol coined the term "kleptomania" (stealing insanity) to describe the behaviors of several kings who stole worthless items. Both Pinel and Esquirol seemed to be commenting on a person's ability to appear normal with the exception of perhaps one or two deviant behaviors.

However, over the years it became clear that those suffering from kleptomania displayed not only stealing behavior, but a variety of possibly associated signs and symptoms. As we have seen, the vast majority of kleptomaniacs clearly suffer from symptoms of chronic depression and anxiety. Could Mrs. Leigh-Perrot's "reserved" demeanor have been depression?

Depression was clearly an issue in Susan's case. Initially, she discussed symptoms of chronic depression, emptiness, and anxiety. Most notable about her depression was that it was not, for the most part, a response to anything she could identify.

I have found this "long-term," smoldering depression to be present in the majority of my patients suffering from kleptomania. Rather than being a recent phenomena— or in response to a known loss or other recent problem— Susan's depression and despair appeared to be rooted in her early developmental years. It seems likely that the origins of her depression—and (most likely) her stealing behavior— represent the consequences of a longstanding, deeply ingrained emotional conflict.

Kleptomaniacs may suffer from many other problems, of which depression and anxiety are only a few. Many researchers have noticed a link between eating disorders and kleptomania. In a review of cases, McElroy and colleagues found kleptomania in twenty-one percent of 719 people with eating disorders. The majority of my own patients have manifested various forms of eating disorders as well. While the nature of the relationship between eating disorders and kleptomania is still unclear, there are indications that people who steal and have eating disorders may be prone to other, more severe, emotional difficulties.

In addition to depression, anxiety, and eating disorders, some kleptomaniacs may also come from tumultuous homes, be socially isolated, or have either disturbed marital relations, poor self-esteem, or sexual problems. Pervasive suicidal feelings are also quite common. There is also evidence that dissociation (a feeling of detachment from one's self or reality) may also be present. Some researchers feel that this state of dissociation is inevitably present during theft. I feel it far more important that there are reports of dissociation in their everyday lives, not merely while they are in the act of stealing.

KLEPTOMANIA'S RELATIONSHIP TO PERSONALITY DISORDERS

We have already looked at the issue of antisocial personality and its relationship to kleptomania. What about other personality issues? Is stealing in some way related to personality development? A personality disorder is a chronic, maladaptive way of interacting with one's environment. We all have our own specific and unique traits: some helpful, others not. However, those with personality disorders find it difficult to interact smoothly with other people. Meaningful and emotionally mutually satisfying relationships with others may be difficult. There are many classes of personality disorders. People with one particular personality disorder, BPD (borderline personality disorder), and those with kleptomania appear to share some similarities.

According to *DSM-IV*, to carry a diagnosis of BPD, a person must meet five of the following criteria:

• A pattern of unstable and intense interpersonal relationships characterized by alternating between extremes of over-idealization and devaluation.
• Impulsiveness in at least two areas that are potentially self-damaging, such as spending, sex, substance abuse, shoplifting (typically meant to imply ordinary stealing), reckless driving, or binge eating.
• Affective instability: marked shifts from baseline mood to depression, irritability, or anxiety, usually lasting a few hours, but rarely more than a few days.
• Inappropriate, intense anger or lack of control of anger, such as frequent displays of temper, constant anger, or recurrent physical fights.
• Recurrent suicidal threats, gestures, or self-mutilating behavior.
• Marked and persistent identity disturbance manifested by uncertainty about at least two of the following: self-image, sexual orientation, long-term goals or career choices, type of friends desired, or preferred values.
• Chronic feelings of emptiness or boredom.
• Frantic efforts to avoid real or imagined abandonment.

Clearly, most of us, at one time or another, have temporarily met at least some of these criteria, particularly during adolescence or during times of great stress. However, for a patient suffering from BPD, many of these signs and symptoms generally start in early adulthood and are pervasive.

Although many other personality disorders exist (most of us have mild forms of a variety of different personality styles, traits, and even disorders), kleptomania and BPD share some commonalities. Susan felt incapable of interacting with her peers, was dependent on family members, and was moody, irritable, and chronically suicidal. She exhibited rejection sensitivity and often felt betrayed and abandoned by people. Rage, impulsiveness, and feelings of emptiness were perpetual. Paula experienced many disturbing characteristics not wholly inconsistent with borderline traits. She told me, "I used to burn myself with an iron, too. My parents didn't know. They thought that the burns were accidents. I burned myself on the arms and legs. I cut my face once. I have scars from cutting that run up my arms. I actually just burned myself last week."

Could kleptomania be a "symptom" of BPD? Do the two coexist? Since they have so many things in common, should kleptomania be added to the list of criteria for BPD? Not everything about BPD and kleptomania are similar. One of the differences, according to the *DSM-IV* criteria, is the intense anxiety and sense of gratification or relief afforded to the kleptomaniac after stealing. On the other hand, people with BPD frequently cut themselves to relieve anxiety, and often experience gratification and relief in response to the self-cutting. Is there a link? We will approach this later.

A.R. Favazza, in examining possible associations between personality disorders and kleptomania, notes that, "Occasional binge eating or shoplifting episodes, for example, are consonant with the construct of borderline personality disorder, but a pattern of repetitive episodes warrants the additional diagnosis of bulimia nervosa or kleptomania."

BPD is not the only personality disorder possibly related to kleptomania. Compulsiveness, dependency, and histrionic and hysterical presentations also appear from time to time in those with a diagnosis of kleptomania. Unfortunately, since little is known about the vast majority of cases, we must interpret these data with great caution.

Can we make any definitive statements about BPD, other personality disorders, and kleptomania as a single related entity? Unfortunately, there simply is not enough data to make these determinations. We may eventually discover that the signs and symptoms of both personality disorders and kleptomania are built upon the same developmental substratum.

IS KLEPTOMANIA RELATED TO, OR PART OF, A DEPRESSIVE DISORDER?

We know that depression is, in some way, related to kleptomania. Most kleptomaniacs are depressed. However, can we claim that kleptomania is simply a sign or symptom of depression?

McElroy and her associates write that "four lines of evidence suggest that kleptomania may be related to major depression" and also refer to "the high frequency of associated depressive and anxiety symptoms in persons with kleptomania" and "reports of kleptomania behavior alleviating symptoms of major depression." They also cite as evidence the association of kleptomania with eating disorders (which appear related to depression) and of the resolution of kleptomania symptoms in response to antidepressant medications and treatment. However, not all people with depression or kleptomania improve with medication treatment. While it is enticing to include kleptomania as a symptom of major depression, the relationship is probably far more complex.

KLEPTOMANIA'S RELATIONSHIP TO OBSESSIVE-COMPULSIVE DISORDER

Abrahamsen, Laughlin and Jenike's theory holds that kleptomania is a form of, or is related to, obsessive-compulsive disorder. It is clear that theft in kleptomania appears to be repetitive, irresistible, and "meaningless." Noting these qualities, some have suggested that kleptomania may be related to what mental health professionals call "obsessive-compulsive disorder" (OCD). In its most severe form, OCD, an anxiety disorder, can be a serious, extremely uncomfortable disorder. In OCD, a person develops an obsession, which is a recurrent, uncomfortable, intrusive mental event such as a thought or feeling. A compulsion is a consistently recurring behavior, which may occur in response to an obsession.

Typically, a compulsion—such as hand-washing—is undertaken in an attempt to reduce anxiety associated with the obsessive ideas. A person with an obsessive-compulsive disorder would be someone who feels they have left the gas stove ignited and returns to the home again and again to check the problem in order to relieve their anxiety. Despite the fact that the person knows the actions are absurd, they are unable to resist the invading thoughts or behaviors. The entire day may be wasted by doing nothing but returning home to check the stove.

Kleptomania also appears to be repetitive, irresistible, and meaningless. Should it be classified as an obsessive-compulsive disorder? Could the "obsession" be the feeling of tension (needing to take) experienced immediately prior to stealing? Could the act of theft be considered to be a compulsion used to diminish the tension associated with the obsession?

As some researchers have noted, the behavior seen in OCD appears to be not so much an end in itself, but is instead designed by the patient to prevent or produce some future event. Repeatedly checking the stove insures that the house does not burn down: "If I don't check the stove, the house will burn down." In kleptomania, the act of stealing *is* the end. Additionally, unlike behavior seen in OCD, which is unpleasant and disliked by the patient, kleptomania may bring intense gratification. Such gratification is less common, however, than the simple relief of tension seen in OCD.

Some of the observations leading researchers to draw similarities between the two illnesses may also be attributable to treatment issues. For example, medications that help people suffering from OCD may, in some circumstances, help those suffering from kleptomania. The connection between OCD and kleptomania is still to be determined, but these observations speak to the unresolved complexities seen in the disorder.

Despite all our knowledge, it remains to be seen how, if at all, kleptomania is diagnostically related to depression or personality and anxiety disorders. Certainly, to early researchers, kleptomania was the only strange sign or symptom in what seemed an otherwise normal, healthy person. However, we have seen that kleptomania appears to be only the tip of the diagnostic iceberg.

CHAPTER 10

Confessions:
The Secret Life
of the Kleptomaniac

"What if I tell you my name and all my secrets?"
— poetry written by Beth, a patient

Why does Beth need to keep secrets? What role do secrets play in her life? What is the risk in divulging them? To Beth and others like her, the risk is great. By necessity, both personal and diagnostically, the stealing in kleptomania is undertaken in isolation. In fact, much of kleptomania's "benefit," as we will see, comes from its forbidden and secret nature. What prevents the person from disclosing? One reason is self-preservation. In a sense, most kleptomaniacs have an unconscious dialogue with themselves very much like this: "If I reveal my behavior, it won't be a secret anymore. If it's not a secret anymore, then what good is the behavior? Then what do I do? How then can I take care of myself?"

Those with kleptomania may wish to share their

dilemmas, but stop themselves from doing so. As a result of the push to remain silent, both sufferers and their families experience a tremendous sense of painful isolation and loneliness. Lara is one kleptomaniac who finally found her lengthy history of theft too heavy a burden to bear alone. Eventually, she found a reason for disclosure and found it to be liberating.

Despite Lara's disclosure, secrets figure prominently in the lives of kleptomaniacs. In the next few chapters, we will look closely into the lives of several patients, none of whom felt at ease in discussing their problems. Some were ashamed, while others feared legal retaliation. So as not to feel threatened, vulnerable, or exposed, each chose a different way of relating their story. Self-revelation may be extremely helpful, but it is not without its liabilities: telling one's story can be traumatic. Whether or not sufferers have difficulty discussing their problems, stealing signifies a bridge to other deeper, more secretive issues.

The concept of uncovering secrets is central to the psychotherapeutic process. Together, psychotherapists and patients strive to uncover and explore the conscious and unconscious secrets that interfere with the patient's functioning. The power of uncovering secrets has been used in various contexts to help people change lives. Early Protestant ministers, for example, enabled troubled people to rid themselves of disturbing secrets. Moritz Benedickt (one of Freud's influences) described the role of the secret in his discussions concerning the origin of hysteria. He considered the secret invariably sexual. Jung and other psychoanalysts obtained cures by relieving patients of painful secrets through confession. More recently, secrecy (both conscious and unconscious) in the therapeutic setting has attracted interest because of its frequent relationship to child-hood sexual and physical abuse.

There is another interesting perspective regarding the "forfeiture" of part of one's self to another. As children, to break a secret pact with someone was to sever the intimate ties that bound one to another; it most certainly traumatized the relationship. For those suffering from kleptomania, to reveal the secret also represents a trauma with oneself. The secret of kleptomania is like a friend—to share it with others represents a violation of a secret pact one has made with one-self. Some kleptomaniacs probably feel that the relieving qualities of stealing would be lost through such disclosure. Yet, there may be another reason for a person's fear of dis-closing these important details: an unwillingness or inability to trust the world about them.

Divulging details of one's life is important to the therapeutic process, but carries with it a certain danger. The cost of revealing secrets may result in the pain of reliving them, forcing an individual to choose between pain and trusting what he or she perceives as an unforgiving and treacherous world.

STORIES OF KLEPTOMANIA

The intimate revelations of those suffering from kleptomania refute many myths. They reveal real people in emotional turmoil or crisis. Taken from a variety of different individuals, these cases underscore a variety of important topics. While some details have been altered to protect their identities, the basic themes of the patients' stories have been left intact.

Lara's history illustrates the relationship between kleptomania and addictive behavior. It also details a variety of other painful lifetime experiences that ultimately contributed to her kleptomania.

Beth's story is significant because it indicates a kleptomania sufferer's desire to tell her story despite strong social and cultural taboos against engaging in such an exercise. It highlights her psychological associations with stealing in a poetic and narrative form.

Susan's experiences chronicle portions of an ongoing psychotherapy. Throughout the course of treatment, Susan claimed to have many secrets that she was unable to share in therapy. Eventually, many years after starting psychotherapy, she revealed a long history of impulsive theft.

Paula's story reveals many signs and symptoms consistent with kleptomania. Much of Paula's identity is defined by stealing and other self-abusive behaviors. Her thefts also highlight her struggle with self-hatred.

Acknowledgment of kleptomania may well point to other distressing signs and symptoms. For Lara, Beth, Susan, and Paula, kleptomania acted as a sort of "red flag," signaling a host of other problems and difficulties. These patients appear to be driven to steal to fill certain unspecified secret voids or deficits in their lives. Such secrets may be conscious or unconscious. Lara was forced to keep secrets about a variety of issues. Beth has harbored her secret of stealing and other secrets for years. In Susan's case, she made it known that there were many secrets she kept which she could never disclose to me. Paula kept many crucial life issues to herself as she was allowed no avenue for self-revelation and was never believed in any event.

The cases of these four people are also significant because their variety of problems illustrate that kleptomania knows no particular level of emotional health. Some of the individuals who have kleptomania's symptoms appear to be healthy and high-functioning, while others are so ravaged by the torment of ongoing mental illness that they are unable to care for themselves meaningfully.

CHAPTER 11

"I Need to Unburden Myself"

"This is all very scary. It is a secret, and I have had a lot of secrets."

— Lara

Seventy-years-old and fragile looking, Lara's hospital admissions had become more frequent and had taken on a different quality. Her psychiatric symptoms were so severe that she was a suicide risk. As the extent of her despair and anguish increased, neither medications nor psychotherapy seemed to calm her or dissipate her despair. No one seemed to have the ability to get to the roots of her anguish.

Certain clinical facts were known about Lara. Her frequent admissions to hospitals generally centered around her depression. Although she had tried many different antidepressants, nothing seemed to help. She complained of mood swings, sleep disturbances, and chronic migraine headaches. One of her previous admissions was precipitated by an addiction to painkillers taken to relieve her severe headaches. She had a history of alcohol abuse, but took pride in having experienced several years of sobriety. On occasion, she had become psychotic, experiencing hallucinations and delusions.

Lately, however, Lara's condition had worsened. She suffered from virtually continuous migraine headaches, suicidal ideation, sleeplessness, and weight gain. She had been overdosing on the pain medication for her headaches and appeared anxious, frightened, and needy. Her speech was slow and muted. She spoke hesitantly and with caution. Her distress was palpable. She felt alone and despondent.

It was three years before Lara divulged one of her biggest secrets to me, a secret she had kept to herself for decades. She expressed an extraordinary amount of guilt over her behavior and was fearful about discussing it. Despite her fear and reluctance, she told me of her former kleptomania and that she had recently started to steal again.

In discussing theft, Lara spoke slowly and cautiously. She was extremely depressed, almost despondent. When discussing painful memories, Lara often cried and was reluctant to speak. When finally she could bring herself to speak, she explained, "The reason I have agreed to discuss this is to help others like me who suffer from the same obsession and addiction. I also need to finally talk honestly about this, so I can unburden myself. By sharing my big secret with someone I trust, I can be less alone, scared, and ashamed. I hope that, by sharing this, I can stop bouncing from one addiction to the next."

Lara took a deep breath and continued telling me about her long and continued past.

"I started stealing a long time ago. I think I was in my twenties and married. My sister had given me a big gold bag, and I used to take it into the stores and steal food. They had sneakers there, and I'd take them for my children. It is funny, I only remember stealing once as a child. I took a deck of cards. It eventually became an obsession for me. I thought about it all the time—even when I was not stealing. I would think about the next time I would go to the store. I was drinking a lot, too. I started using alcohol at age thirteen. Even back then, I guess I was going from one addiction to the next. I think I have been substituting one addictive behavior for another. When one behavior did not give me what I needed, I would move on to the next. I would steal to make myself feel better. I was getting away with something—doing something that my husband did not know about. He always had the power. He would say to me, 'I hold all the cards.' He would always beat me. Stealing was something I had all to myself.

"Stealing kept me company. It made me feel more equal to my husband in terms of power; I also felt so very ashamed. On the one hand, I needed the behavior, but on the other hand, I beat myself up emotionally about it because stealing is wrong. I grew up thinking and being taught stealing was wrong. I am carrying around an extra burden, and I feel I should go to confession.

"I took stuff I needed and used, but I also took things I did not need at all. I would take candy, and I do not even eat candy. I could not leave the store without taking something. I took just to take. It did not seem right to walk out of a store without stealing. I also took cosmetics and makeup. I would hide it in the house. There would be piles of these things hidden in cupboards and closets. I would usually throw them away. It was the act of taking things that I liked. I would walk in, get the stuff that I had needed, and then take things I did not need. If I left a store without taking, I would feel like I lost out.

"Once I left the store, I got relief. I have always been depressed—since age seven. The last time I felt good was about fifteen years ago. I was living with nuns in a home for women. I was working and addiction free, but I was still stealing.

"My history of trauma goes way back. I lived with my grandparents until I was six. I hated to go home to my parents because my father was so passive, and my mother drank and ignored us children. She would take us in the middle of the night to neighbors while she partied. I had horrible migraines back then, and she never believed me. My father tried to appease her. He did not drink, but just was not there for me. My father was in the service, and, when I was six, my parents took me and my two younger siblings to the Middle East. They used to leave me alone with the two children. My brother was fourteen months old and my sister was four. They would leave me all night. I would get so scared being alone, so scared. I remember the fear. I would wait up for them. I would sit on the bed waiting for them. I got so scared that I once lost my voice for two weeks. I could not take care of them. I just did not have any childhood.

"We came back from the Middle East and went to Japan. I was nine and was starting to develop. I got my period at age nine. I started being promiscuous then. I was not having intercourse, but I would let boys kiss and touch me. I did it because I was looking for love in all the wrong places. I was looking for something to help me feel good about myself, but it made me feel rotten. Just like stealing. I knew it was wrong, but I did it anyway because I knew there was something in my body that someone wanted. I felt rejected by my parents, and I was searching for other experiences to make me feel more whole, more of a person.

"When I was eleven, I was going out with men older than me. That is when I started having intercourse, and it was for the same reason. I was having intercourse with adults. It was truly an abusive situation. This makes me remember that I was abused as a child as well. A friend of my mother would take me into the greenhouse. He would pull down my panties and touch me down there and put his mouth there and play with me. I was really young: he was an older man. I was scared to tell my mother because I was afraid she would not believe me, just like with the headaches. She never believed that I was ever in any kind of pain or distress. I kept everything to myself. I had a lot of secrets. My mother would tell me not to tell my father about her affairs. I have felt guilty all my life. I have felt different all my life and never felt like I belonged. I still don't.

"I met my ex-husband. He used to take me out drinking. I was thirteen then. He was twenty-three. It was a big difference. I started to drink heavily. My poor father tried to help me. He was overwhelmed and could not take care of me and my mother. I got engaged when I was fourteen. My father was upset, but he did not say anything. He just shook his head. I am furious with him because he did not stop me. My then fiancé went back to the States, and I started to see other men. I kept it a secret. I think my father knew, but he did not say anything. My experience with these other men was similar to my other experiences with stealing and alcohol. I needed it, but felt terribly guilty about it. I wanted to go to my mother so badly for her help, but could not.

"I had a good body, and I had something to use, something that somebody wanted. I did not always look like this. I was fifteen and still engaged. We started to plan the wedding. I am very angry that my father let me get married. It would have been nurturing if he had forbidden it, but I guess God wanted me to have five children. We got married, and he started beating me right from the first. I wanted a baby badly, something for me to love. I never loved him like a woman should love a man. Having sex was. . . . I cried—I just wanted it over. I did not want it, so I drank a lot. I got pregnant at seventeen. My husband was transferred to Korea. I was so scared. I felt so alone, like I did when I had to take care of my siblings way back. I even felt alone when I was with other people. Our living quarters were dirty and cold. I had the baby, and my husband took over right away. It was like she was not mine. I was drinking a lot and got pregnant again. I still was not stealing. My husband was beating me constantly.

"My life was so stressful. I had three kids in Korea and I was just twenty-one. I did not know what to do with these three kids. We returned to the States, and I got pregnant again. My husband's family were all around, but they would not help me with the shopping or anything. They used to follow me around in a car. They considered me a sinner because I was from the West Coast. I guess I was a sinner.

"I was in my twenties when my mother was murdered. She was forty-two and had gotten in with the wrong crowd. I was pregnant and could not go to the funeral. Nobody in my family will tell me what happened. My father died of a massive heart attack six months before my mother died. When my mother died, it killed me. I went stark raving mad. I should have been hospitalized. I should have been put somewhere. But I had my bottle and I had my men. I can remember sitting alone on my bed all night, clutching my bottle, talking to it, saying, 'You are my only friend.'

"I was in my twenties when I started to steal. I was doing a lot of drinking. I was also using street drugs. My husband bought them for me despite his disapproval. It was his way of having the power over me. He always called me 'the sick one.' If I was messed up, he had the power over me. I was taking a lot of stuff. I started taking the stuff because I needed it, but then I started taking things that I did not need or use. What was pleasurable about stealing was the challenge. I got caught, though. I guess the store owners had been observing me for a while. I wondered why they would let me get away with the stealing if they had been observing me. They took me up to the office and were going to call the police. I cried. I cried that I could not take this. They made me promise that I would never come back into the store, and they let me go. I never went back there, but I went to other stores and started all over again. It did not deter me. I just never went back to that store.

"After sixteen years I was divorced on grounds of desertion. I was so sick with my alcoholism, and I felt that I was destroying my children. He was a terrible person for a husband, but I thought he was a good father and I walked out. I just could not take the beatings any more. I left the children with him. That was the worst thing I could have done. I still feel guilty over that. I was still stealing and drinking more. I went into a detox and met a woman there. We stayed together for seven years, and during that time I do not think I was stealing that much. They were not good years for me. I had the problem with sex, and after the third year, I stopped all sex. I felt so guilty. We drank on and off. I have been sexually numb since.

"I thought I would try to live the good life again. I met this man in detox. This was a disaster. He was an alcoholic and beat me so bad. I was with him on my fortieth birthday and I looked around—we were living in this dirty old room—and I said, 'Is this all there is?' and I went out and got drunk. I left him, went to a detox, and then to a halfway house run by nuns. This was in the early eighties. I was not drinking, so I was not getting into trouble. I am a vicious, vicious drunk—like the devil incarnate. Punching, kicking, fighting, biting. Although I was still depressed, these years were relatively better. I was living with nuns in a residence for women. You needed to be working. You got your meals and your own room. It was very nice. I was there for seven years. I was surrounded by morality—a concept I had been struggling with all my life. Even when I was living at the residence, I was stealing, but not as much. I was using codeine at the time for my headaches. The stealing started up again even though I had a job and was given my meals. I would take perfume.

"But, all of a sudden, I got very, very ill. I started having anxiety attacks, and I was very depressed. It all caught up with me. Everything hit me all at once. I started seeing psychiatrists and going into hospitals. My suicidal feeling got strong. I have always been suicidal and have made dozens of attempts. The first attempt was when I was married. I almost died. I took a huge amount of pills. I have even jumped out of cars. I have had the very strong feeling that I do not want to be here. I cut myself. I used to cut myself a lot. It would take the other pain away. It would give me a sense of peace and relief. It was a good kind of pain, a better pain than what I was going through inside. It was a distraction.

"The stealing had been painful, not only for me, but for the important people around me. At first, my partner did not know I was doing it because I would hide everything. Eventually, though, she would always find it. It drove her crazy. I would put piles of makeup in a hiding place—more makeup than I could possibly ever use. I was always going to wear it, but I never did.

"I am very ashamed of this. It goes against every-thing I believe in. Stealing is wrong. When I was drinking or using drugs, I knew it was wrong, but I did it anyway. Whenever I see anything on television about people who get caught stealing, I understand. I understand. This is all very scary. It is a secret, and I have had a lot of secrets. I have taken things from restaurants—salt and pepper shakers and napkins. I would not really use them. I need to stop for me. It is like I need to be drug-free."

ONGOING THEMES

For Lara, stealing is torture, but it represents a com-promise between feeling completely out of control and being depressed. Clearly, Lara's childhood was short-lived. Plagued by the tumult around her, she suffered in silence, carrying secrets and fear. Forced to "grow up" quickly, she cast aside the normal childhood experiences and replaced them with behaviors that even an adult would find challenging. At the age of six, she was forced to care for her younger siblings, while her promiscuous mother used alcohol irresponsibly. Her father, resented by Lara for his lack of boundary setting, was absent as well. She suffered physical and sexual assaults and had no support system.

Not surprisingly, in an attempt to search for love and affection, Lara herself developed habits that made her feel out of control. Alcohol and drug use, promiscuity, and an early marriage to an abusive, older man placed her at an even greater risk of acting out her despair. All of these "vices," however, were not without great emotional cost. Lonely, guilt-ridden, depressed, anxious, and suicidal, Lara found her life intolerable. She developed severe headaches and a variety of other somatic difficulties, including obesity. In addition, she had severe sexual identity confusion.

Lara's story depicts a lifelong search for meaning, control, and a feeling of "wholeness." By running from one self-destructive habit to the next, she was trying to free herself from immorality while, at the same time, searching for ways to soothe herself. For Lara, theft was simply another way of acting out or expressing her inner turmoil. She agreed with my observation that, for her, stealing was a distraction. She explained, "It is something I do to try to make myself feel better than I am feeling. I get kind of excited about it. It is a challenge. It makes me nervous. Then, like all the other things, it makes me feel as if I had violated a code of morality. Then I end up feeling worse. It is like sex and drinking and using drugs and cutting. It feels good at that moment, and then afterward I do not feel so good."

Lara seemed to recognize the relationship between self-destructive behavior and the temporary relief it offers. Yet she continued to steal. Let us continue to build upon the themes present in her story by examining several others in people suffering from kleptomania.

CHAPTER 12

"Sometimes I Dream About Stealing"

"Sometimes I dream about stealing. I take something. I am always so glad when I resist in the dream. When I wake up, I know it is not over. . . ."

– Beth

For some individuals, the worst part of kleptomania is the fear of apprehension; for others, it is the humiliation. For many, the violation of societal ethical codes is intolerable. Guilt and remorse become overwhelming. While the act of stealing may offer short-term relief, many are so tortured by their own violations that any relief brought by the act itself is immediately lost to remorse and self-loathing.

Although filled with self-hatred and hesitant to discuss her difficulties, dark-haired and pretty-faced Beth agreed to tell her story and some of her feelings because she felt that, in doing so, she could help others. She said she was both baffled and devastated by her own behavior. "Let me use

the ugliest and most honest words to describe what I sometimes do, and what I always loathe myself for. Let me use the
most brutal and clearest words to try to cut open what infects,
so that I cannot kid myself that it is something else."

As with most who later develop kleptomania, Beth
said her first experience seemed little more than ordinary
theft: "Chronologically, the first time I recall taking something was taking a book once in undergraduate school when
I was packing for a vacation and a trip to the library seemed
just too much to handle."

The next time Beth stole was several years later:

"I took money from a dresser drawer of my grand-
mother. I was visiting with a young man I planned to marry,
but that very morning we peaceably decided not to. To
marry him would have meant being married outside my
faith, and I did not want to do that. Someone else was
blamed for the theft. I lied about it. I was ashamed and
remember it clearly. I cannot recall the 'why' in this case.
Money was tight. I felt separated both from the young man
and from my grandparents to whom I could not tell the
truth—mainly about Tom (who was later killed in combat
while serving in the Navy) or about the money."

Beth continues with a statement about her painfully
ambivalent feelings.

"I think there was anger there at the separation from
the young man. Although I was peaceful about the decision,
it still hurt in some ways.

"Somewhere in the same time frame I took three

dollars from the purse of a friend. It was sitting on the kitchen table. I do not know why. I felt filthy. Dante has the lowest circle of Hell for those who betray their friends.

"Several years later, I got married, quit work after the birth of my son, and eventually stayed home to keep the house and rear my four sons and daughter. When I had been married about ten years, I had an affair with my husband's cousin. Although he had a number of personal problems, we had always liked each other. Although it might have nothing to do with stealing, I think it might. During the affair, I did not steal anything.

"My husband and I entered therapy together, but decided not to continue the marriage. I was so depressed that I started on an antidepressant. It was the first time in years I realized how low I felt—because I could make a comparison with feeling half-human.

"One very painful part of my life was my lack of a relationship with my father. From the time I was a sophomore in high school until a year before he died when I was in my early forties, my father refused to speak with me. The only thing he would say to me was that I was 'no good.' As a teenager, I experienced strong emotional stress in relation to my father. I did not understand it, because I was the quintessential good kid. I got decent grades, had no real hassles with my parents as I grew up, and succumbed to their strict rules. I was not allowed to date, I did chores, and I did not sneak out for dates or drinks.

"My father and I had a misunderstanding about a time when I was supposed to be in after a youth activity. My cousin and I came in late, around 11:00 P.M. In the verbal exchange that followed, he grounded me and ventured that he could not trust me, and (as they say) that was that. From that point on, he never talked to me, ignored me at the dinner table and other places. The most he would ever say to me when I tried to clarify things to him about my being late was that I was not what he expected. I should add here that, during my last year in college, I disobeyed my mother and father in a significant way. My father was a very important eye surgeon in town. None of us siblings had had an eye exam in years, and I had difficulty with my vision, which I had told him about a year before. So, after my vision worsened, I got the advice of a professor at my college and quietly obtained the surgery I needed in order not to embarrass my family. The eye surgeon promised secrecy and kept his word. I slowly paid off the bill.

"As it turned out, my sister had developed the same eye disorder. I begged her to have it taken care of, and that I would help pay for it. Despite the fact that she was almost totally blind in one eye, she refused because it would mean disobeying our parents, who would then become angry with her.

"My mother was mainly a peacekeeper. She tried to avoid conflict. She is a good person and in many ways is quite strong. She intervened in a few ways to relieve pressure and has said that, in the few major confrontations with my father, she always lost.

"While I was a college student, someone suggested that I pray for my father—not for what it would do for him, but because of what it would do for me. I was hoping that prayer would help me from closing up altogether. I have found that to be good advice. The brief end to the story is that I made a number of attempts at reconciliation after I left home. To support myself, I became a companion for an elderly couple in exchange for room and board. One of my parents biggest worries was 'what would people think?' about me leaving home. Many years later, in part because of the work with a therapist (who told me I needed to stop running), my father 'let' me come home. My then husband was very supportive, and we all visited my parents. After that, my dad would never discuss what had happened, or how he felt or anything. He communicated by repairing things for me and making toys for my children. He was very meticulous. I accepted his style and found lines of communication in some shared interests. Still, I have found myself a little wary sometimes, although I did not want to be, and when we visited (not often, because of the distance) I would get exhausted listening to him talk. He just wanted someone to listen. He died about three years ago, and my sister and I experienced the same sense of sorrow and loss and the ability to forgive.

"In my early twenties and later, I had suicidal ideas, but no gestures, save once when I took some sleeping pills, but only enough to sleep. It was both a deliberate, desperate wanting to die, and a decision not to. I think the thing that stopped me was not fear of the unknown, nor of punishment, but that killing myself would not be congruent with trying to live a life of faith.

"Later, after my separation, I stole something from the store where my then husband worked. I do not recall what it was. The problem has been with me ever since. It comes and goes. No, maybe more accurately, sometimes I do and sometimes I do not. Usually postcards from art museums. Magazines. Sometimes books. Cards. Useful to me, but not needed. Shuffled in with things I have paid for.

"These are all the things that are most important to me: communication, learning, design, sharing. And stealing associated with them corrupts them. And sometimes there is a sneaky satisfaction, a sort of ugly glee.

"I don't plan to. Sometimes it is over before I know what has happened. Sometimes I know that I will even when I say that I won't.

"Sometimes I have thought about going to the manager of a store when I enter and say, 'Look, watch me. I could steal you blind. Help me. Watch me. I do not want to.' But I never do. Sometimes I think about getting caught and the consequences. And then: blank. I 'forget' until I look back in horror and satisfaction. Well, that is the ugly truth. And then the desolation, the utter 'Oh, no, not again! I will not do that again.' Sometimes I start to take something and then put it down. I will not, I will not. It is just like Jacob wrestling with some perverted angel. A siege: Masada, Leningrad. Sometimes I just do not go into a store where I know I can steal. Or stay away from the tempting department. Or, I just put cash and my driver's license in my pocket and go into the store with no purse in which to hide something.

"Is it associated with my feeling about money in general? I do not think I handle money well. Sometimes I put off paying bills until I am at a crisis level. I borrowed some money not yet paid back. I could manage money better. Buy fewer books. Budget. But no matter what, things are tight. There are no pensions, no savings. I get scared. The car has 171,000 miles on it. Not as an excuse do I say this—just to say that sometimes the pressures are relentless. When the kids are finally gone, I would like to serve as a volunteer to people really in need. That's long been a dream. I would like to have the time to write. But money, unpaid bills, spending too much are a source of great anxiety.

"I now work full-time in a demanding job I do not like. I think the company is not entirely honest, and they treat their employees poorly. Much pressure to reach 'goals.'

"Why do I keep on stealing when I do not want to, or say I do not want to? Something is askew. I can't get at it. I have gone to confession and been direct and finally was told not to confess it. It was not under my control, a compulsion.

"Did I perhaps read too much Marx in college, and somehow identify with the exploited, and figure I can revolt? My logical mind knows better, my moral upbringing and belief and standards will not buy that (buy, isn't that an incongruous word!) but somehow this is not logic.

"I feel as though I want to cry at this writing.

"Sometimes the stealing is associated with design. The design, the artistic merit is good, and I want it and cannot otherwise have it. Sometimes I need two of something so that I can share it, but can only afford one. So I steal. I spend a lot on photocopying to share articles and other things with friends. Mom says I am like dad—interested in many things, with a good eye—creative. But I do not hold a grudge. Except maybe in my dark heart, and I do not want to hold them there.

"Is it lack of impulse control? Am I proving my father right, that I am/was no good? Actually, I am good. That is how people see me, and I know I want to be—nothing glamorous—just small kindness and hanging in, especially with my kids for the long haul.

"The first time a person breaks a rule or a taboo, he or she looks up in amazement that the skies have not thundered and the world come to an end. Then you discover that the rule or taboo or 'thou shalt not' can be broken and nothing will happen. At least maybe. Something happens inside though. Do you rot or become injured or what?

"Once, while I was watching my sister's children, one of my nephews was caught stealing. I had to go to court. I admonished him, but when it was over, it was over. My daughter was caught once as well. I always argue furiously when one of my kids does not understand that it is wrong to steal. In no case, though, did I ever tell anyone involved about the thorn in my side. Hypocrite? Maybe, yes. When one of my sister's kids shoplifted, I did speak with her and told her that I steal, although I did not tell her how recently. I just wanted to reach out to her in the feelings and the reality and mainly be a connection.

"There are rules about stealing. Not from friends. Not from some place important to me. Not in anyone's house. Just from the capitalist bastards? Just from the exploiters? Just what I need? Do not sully some place. Do not soil your own bed. Do not despoil a place. But, then, if I do well, then the taboo is breached, it does not matter anymore.

"Is it to prove I am alive? Is it like pressing, pressing, pressing against an aching tooth for the moment's relief? I have had some horrendous bouts with depression. When I become overwhelmed by depression, I cannot focus, and I cannot process fast enough. I need quiet and time alone. Then I might steal something. Sometimes I resist, but at this point the thought comes to mind much too often. In some ways, the stealing is the same. I do not quite know the connection; it is as though it holds something at bay. What monster, what incubus? Will I need greater and greater means to hold it at bay? The 'it' is not the stealing. It is something else, and I do not know what.

"For several blocks of time about ten or twelve years ago when I was teaching, I would get home from school, take care of the kids (homework, chauffeuring, just talking) and then, as I started to fix dinner, I would also fix myself a drink, sometimes two. We had our meal, and the evening went on as usual. I do not think I took anything then. I just wondered if there could be a connection, because the patterns are similar. Blocks of a given activity, and then nothing. I am not sure that the "fixing the drink" block of activity had the same degree of compulsion as the taking seems to, and fixing a drink on occasion does not, at this point, preclude the other unfortunately—or else I would just settle in with the Wild Turkey and a good book! But I just wonder. The pattern of a drink every night became clear to me back then and I quit—and started, and quit.

"Could there be a shift (at least at some time periods, with other time periods free of this shift) to going some place to take something rather than it 'happening?' And, at other times, it is 'just happening.' I take something without the intention? I picture an interior with the face of a Scrooge, pulling into himself with a greedy 'Heh, heh, heh' and a 'wringing' of hands, while the public face is normal. Just an image, but that is what it looks like. It seems—it is!—all the more frightening than even the 'plain' taking because it seems a shift to evil and a shift to being all the more out of control. I really do not think of this horrible affliction in 'moral' terms, but, at this moment, I cannot think of a strong enough word otherwise.

"The very worst part of stealing is that I have not lived in accordance with how I want to live, which is with integrity. No 'psychological' or emotional reason, no excuse,

no explanation mitigates that. Upon reflection, I am horrified
by the consequences of getting caught. The best part of
stealing is the emotional thrill of 'getting even, taking back.'
Getting something I need or want momentarily, and that I
'deserve' to be satisfied. It is a pretty mixed 'best' though.

"I would like to say, I would like to think, that stealing
is not concomitant with who I really am, and in some ways I
am afraid, really afraid, that it is. Sometimes I feel as though I
present a false face to others, but I don't want to. I remind
myself, symbolically, that Jesus was crucified next to two
thieves, and one of them we have come to call 'the good thief.'
This is maybe the worst aspect of stealing. I am so sullied that
I have a hard time praying. I want to pray, to be in communication, to offer my whole self to the Lord, and this makes me
ashamed. I want to turn away, to run away. I keep coming back,
I keep believing, I keep reaching out to touch the hem of His
garment. This is a true affliction of hemorrhage."

ONGOING THEMES

Beth's story reveals just how tortured she feels. She
struggles to make sense of her despair and misery. She asks
questions. Her case, among other things, captures much of
what we have outlined up to now—secrecy, despair, depression, aloneness, guilt, and chronic confusion about who she
is. Also chronicled poignantly and candidly is the lack of
empathy during childhood, remorse, and a feeling of dread in
what the individual feels is an ongoing struggle to view as
moral. Beth, like Lara, struggles with the notion of kleptomania as a habit, an uncontrollable addictive-like behavior
that consumes.

CHAPTER 13

Coping With a Troubled Past

"I would rather die than divulge certain things."
– Susan

How hard is it for people to disclose the past? Let us consider Susan, who divulged her stealing only after years of therapy. Susan entered treatment with the unwritten commitment to tolerate the emotional pain that frequently accompanies the insights and memories generated by therapy. Her words came slowly, but they now provide us with an opportunity to analyze her life in great detail. When work was begun, she was guarded and cautious. Her initial reluctance to disclose details of her life is consistent with the secretive nature of kleptomania.

In long-term, dynamic psychotherapy, an alliance between the patient and therapist must be formed before work can be done. This alliance develops as the therapist is able to help the patient create an environment suitable for

trust. Best thought of as the patient's "healthy" self being able
to work with the therapist, this alliance is a powerful tool in
the therapeutic process. Because of the alliance, Susan's
resistance was finally overcome.

SUSAN'S STORY

Susan, a forty-seven-year-old, single woman, began
working in therapy with me in order to get help for a variety
of issues. She initially complained of a twenty-year history of
gradually increasing social isolation and chronic depression.
However, what was really bothering her was her memory. She
was bewildered because, despite her excellent powers of rec-
ollection, she was unable to recall the first fourteen years of
her life, the years her father was in the home. Describing her
depression, she stated that she often felt irritable and was
unable to stabilize her moods, which fluctuated greatly during
the day. She has a quick temper and was upset by small things.
Furthermore, Susan complained of frequent suicidal feelings,
making frequent threats to follow through on her desire to cut
herself or overdose on medications.

During therapy, I noticed that she was able to express
a variety of moods and feelings (such as humor and sadness)
only with great effort. Susan was generally constricted, her
voice being monotone in nature. This lack of emotion persisted throughout therapy. Indeed, her descriptions of significant life events, including both exciting and terrible times,
were related with little emotion. Although she initially
claimed to have almost no childhood memories, an older
male cousin (who had lived with her family since his parents
were killed shortly after his birth) provided her with many

historical details. The remainder surfaced during the course of therapy.

The product of an uncomplicated pregnancy, Susan walked and talked at the appropriate ages. Her biological mother left the home shortly after her birth. The responsibility for raising her was left to the father's girlfriend, with whom he had been having an affair at the time of Susan's birth. The woman eventually married Susan's father. Susan considered the woman to be her "mother" and referred to her as such during the course of therapy.

Susan was a demanding baby, who cried and screamed often. Her screams were so violent that her "mother" would stand outside the house to make it clear to the neighbors that she wasn't beating the child. As she grew older, Susan became an outgoing child, who enjoyed the company of her father's extended family. She also described herself as being obstinate and demanding, often being punished in school and at home for her difficult attitudes and behaviors. Before the family moved to a poor rural community, they lived in a dangerous inner city area, where Susan felt unprotected. She was often teased and beaten by neighborhood children for being taller than other children her age. She was also taunted and viciously struck by her cousin. This ongoing abuse was sanctioned by her "mother," who claimed that Susan was impossible to handle. Susan described one episode where she felt strangely detached from herself during a violent fight with her cousin.

During therapy, Susan stated that her parents were oblivious to her almost constant emotional pain and feelings of vulnerability. Her father, a mechanic, was absent much of the time. Susan described him as addicted to drugs and untrustworthy. Due to constant marital conflict and her father's drug habit and infidelity, Susan's home life was tumultuous. Windows were often closed so that the neighbors could not hear the violent fights. Susan was told not to talk to anyone about her problems or about family turmoil.

Susan reportedly did well in school, but soon became truant. At age fourteen she was placed in parochial school. About that time, her father and "mother" were divorced. As she grew older, she smoked marijuana with her friends, but stopped in her early twenties. Romantic relationships were totally absent from her discussion of this period of her life.

After graduating from high school, Susan continued to live with her "mother." Due to financial pressures, she was unable to attend college. Around the age of twenty she began to withdraw socially. She ceased attending family functions and isolated herself by staying at home on weekends. In her job as a probation officer, she became nasty and hostile to coworkers. She also became moody and tense with anger. Additionally, she developed frequent suicidal thoughts.

In the ensuing years, Susan became more isolated and more preoccupied with death. She continued to work, but rarely ventured outside. Her "mother," alarmed at her unhappiness and isolation, finally insisted she see a therapist, and Susan reluctantly agreed. After a brief period of psychotherapy with a minister (which, according to Susan, "failed to produce any positive results"), she began treatment with me.

It became apparent in the first months of therapy that Susan was an unstable person who had difficulty containing her rage and feelings of betrayal. She exhibited severe mood swings in the office. Although she obtained a modest benefit from a trial of antidepressant medication, she continued to feel abandoned and rejected by those around her. Many of our initial discussions focused on her anger toward her parents for their lack of empathy. She felt that they were not interested in understanding her problems. Susan was a provocateur in therapy and often threatened to commit suicide if I didn't help her quickly. Her ability to free-associate, or to say what she was thinking, was initially limited. Her early statements regarding her dreams and fantasies were vague and cryptic. She remained guarded and secretive about most personal aspects of her life.

Despite continued criticism of therapy, she did not miss a single session and came even when she was sick. However, her rage and suicidal ideation persisted, especially after breaks in therapy. She responded with ridicule and anger to any early attempts to relate her feelings of deprivation. Her rage toward others led to similar feelings directed toward me. Despite her continued and apparent disdain for therapy, however, two major themes emerged early in treatment: her lengthy silences and her painful ambivalence regarding her father.

Susan's silence was the most striking aspect of her participation in therapy. Though mostly mute, she frequently hinted that she had many secrets she could not share with me. Initially, she minimized these secrets, indicating that they were too silly to share. Even though she had an intellectual understanding of therapy and the importance of saying what was on her mind, Susan felt that one wasn't supposed to discuss private matters with anyone. Actually, she had been taught this attitude by her family.

Although she seemed uncomfortable with the sessions,

she acknowledged that there were things to be discussed, but, for many reasons, she was unable to do so. She continued to give hints of secrets and to shift the burden of their revelation to me—blaming me for her own inability to disclose.

In her second year of therapy, Susan revealed more of herself, especially her feelings of betrayal, but she continued to harbor secrets. She would clench her fists and hug herself around the chest whenever the subject of our therapeutic relationship arose. She felt that I was ignoring her needs, and that I was planning to discontinue her treatment. However, at the same time, she feared dependency and further self-revelation. Despite the growing comfort she was gaining from therapy, she still felt inhibited when speaking about personal matters, particularly those related to her therapeutic relationship with me. She would often say, "I guess there are things I want to say, but I don't know how far to go with it."

Susan was eventually able to admit that she had felt depression for more than twenty years, but that she had never felt comfortable telling me about it. Her ability to connect her physical symptoms to psychological states improved, and she became better at self-observation. She wondered why I would want her for a patient and commented that events from her past prevented her from "needing" anyone.

At the same time, Susan expressed anger over things I said or did that disappointed her. However, her healthy observing half commented that perhaps she was using her anger as an excuse not to go forward. She stated that she could not let anyone, including me, get close to her. She continued to express her difficulty in allowing people to know her or to know certain things about her. During therapy, she allowed that she had not told me much, but it was still more than anyone else knew about her. But she still refused to divulge certain things about herself to me.

Toward the end of the second year, Susan developed positive but ambivalent feelings about me. It soon became clear that our therapy sessions represented her first meaningful long-term relationship, and she again stated that she had shared more with me than anyone else.

Susan remained secretive, but admitted feeling fear about continuing her therapy. She told how this feeling appeared to be linked to a recent dream: "I was in my bedroom, and a religious man was standing at the door. I told him it was the wrong room, but he said, 'No.' I screamed for my mother, but she didn't come. I ran out of the room when he put his hands on me. His intentions weren't good."

In subsequent sessions, Susan began to discuss her distrust of men, but she appeared to shut down when the clinical material became too frightening. Her silence bothered her to the point where she considered terminating therapy. I asked her if there was ever a time when she was told to keep silent about something. She became quite agitated and dissociated, feeling as if she was becoming detached from herself. She spoke slowly about her inability to trust. She described her frequent use of dissociation to rid herself of intrusive, frightening thoughts, particularly those related to her negative experiences as a child.

Susan found herself plagued by self-doubt. She assumed that her frightening images and feelings were related to something her father may have done to her, but that they could not be true. She appeared anxious and indicated that she was going to crack her teeth from tension if she was not careful. She eventually disclosed that her father had recently been discussing his sex life with her, and she recognized it as an inappropriate act. During this time, she perceived me as both a caring, empathic parent who could protect her and as a sadist who traumatized her by forcing her to relive her past.

A subsequent session found Susan struggling with "images and fantasies." When I asked if the images were of a sexual nature, she experienced an anxiety attack, causing her to become agitated and extremely nervous. She began to discuss her rage at her father for his untrustworthiness. She stated that, if she ever had children, she would never allow him to "do what he did to me—screw me up! I hated the way he made me feel. Why can't I just dump him?"

Susan later reported a dream about her landlord removing things from boxes in the basement. She shook her head as she remembered the dream: "He wasn't supposed to remove them and had a dumb look on his face like he had done a good job. It gave me the feeling that I had lost it. He had the look my father gets when he feels good about something. In the dream, the landlord looked as though he had just done something wonderful. He was proud of himself."

Susan then discussed her anger at her father's violation of a court order during her childhood. She related feelings of guilt at not seeing him more, but also expressed outrage because her father had betrayed her trust by telling others personal information she had discussed with him in confidence.

Eventually, Susan tried to draw lines. She talked about her need to censor her thoughts and feelings and discussed the dangers of getting into such forbidden territory. During these discussions, she began to adapt self-soothing body movements. Any attempt on my part to classify an issue, however, was still met with silence.

During the summer, Susan informed me at the last minute that it would be necessary for her to miss a great many therapy sessions. She stated that she had some annoying personal medical problems. She had known about the problems for months, but had kept them a secret.

At the end of her second year of therapy, Susan abruptly announced that she was scheduled for surgery for another very personal medical problem and would be absent for several months. She also first revealed that she had had an eating disorder, bulimia, for many years.

Many of the emotional themes of Susan's first two-and-a-half years of therapy seemed related to her father, and they varied greatly. She initially perceived me as an untrustworthy, unemphatic, and, at times, sadistic father. She associated my intrusions with her father, with whom she was afraid to be alone. She felt angry with herself for not being able to get rid of him (me) and could not understand what she needed from him. She predicted that I would betray her just as her father had.

Once Susan described a dream in which she was being pursued by two rapists. In discussing the dream, she soon began to talk about her father, who, while intoxicated, had recently invited her out for a drink. She recalled childhood memories of her intoxicated father lying around the house in the nude: "When I was eight, I awoke to find my father, drugged out, kneeling at my bed. He was trying to hug me, but he was breaking my arm. I was crying. He told me he loved me. I could see my mother standing at the door, crying. I blame my mother for not getting me away from him." Regardless, Susan returned from a vacation with her father later in the month and reported having a good time.

Susan claimed that her inability to discuss certain matters with me was related to my gender. She reiterated her inability to trust her father, who had recently been pressing her to use drugs with him—an activity Susan considered seductive and symbolic of previous inappropriate behaviors. The recollections of these actions made her feel anxious and guilty.

Susan slowly began to understand her dependence upon and passive longings for her father and therapist. As a result, she felt increasingly humiliated and enraged. She wondered how she could have "ended up this way," despite being her father's "favorite person" and receiving special attention from him. She revealed that, as a child, she was "good" to her father because she feared that he would abandon her.

At the beginning of her third year of therapy, Susan claimed that she would rather die than tell me certain things. Over the next few months, her attitude about life seemed to change. She spoke at length about plans to move out of her mother's house, but was overwhelmed by guilt about the action. She realized that she and her mother were extremely dependent on each other. She also felt that her father would never change his insensitive and inappropriate behavior. Yet she reported getting along with him.

Susan finally appeared to be developing a capacity for mutuality in therapy. During our conversations, she had learned how to achieve a relationship with another person. For example, after we had both made concessions regarding a new meeting time for therapy, she finally informed me that, since childhood, she had stolen items of little value. She described her theft of magazines she did not read, candy she would discard, as well as "things so small and insignificant, I don't even remember what they were." Her first act of theft had involved purchasing milk for her mother and pocketing the change. She had felt entitled to take things without paying for them, and often, discarded the item once she had left the store.

Even though her stealing had decreased over the past two years, Susan was still terrified of being caught. She found telling me of these experiences very embarrassing. She felt that the stealing was beyond her control. Nonetheless, she enjoyed the sense of triumph over "getting away with it" when she left the store with a stolen item—even though the act was accompanied by feelings of terror.

After these disclosures, Susan indicated that there were other things she had to tell me, but had not been able. She began discussing issues of intimacy and dependency with greater ease. For the first time, she spoke about men and her inability to achieve intimacy. She still harbored feelings of distrust toward me, accusing me of withholding valuable information from her regarding her treatment—an interesting notion, since it was she who had been withholding information from me. She indicated a desire to flee from my office and intrusions, even while she was expressing positive feelings for me. However, she was able to discuss her ambivalence about me and other men with insight. She reported feelings of tension and competition toward her mother.

During the first two-and-a-half years of therapy, Susan had concealed many secrets, both conscious and unconscious. Often, she consciously suppressed thoughts and feelings which she was unable to share with me. She felt that they might lead to humiliation, judgment, or pain. In part, her inability to discuss certain subjects appeared to be a learned response to a threatening experience: she had been forbidden to discuss feelings about her tumultuous family life with those outside the family. However, by disclosing her conscious secret of kleptomania, she felt less fearful of revealing other conscious secrets.

Since Susan spent great amounts of time discussing what she could not tell me, her secrets had obviously been a defense she used against positive transference toward me—namely, discussing such issues as intimacy, dependency and unacceptable fantasies. As these disclosures appear, they can now be treated adequately in her ongoing therapy.

Despite her insistence that I must find her temperament difficult and her silences boring, the provocative manner in which Susan harbored her secrets served as a seductive technique to keep me interested in her. The secrets served as both conscious and unconscious indications that, if I exhibited patience, I would surely be rewarded.

Despite her fear of arrest and humiliation for her stealing behavior, however, she still consistently refused a different treatment approach for her ongoing kleptomania.

ONGOING THEMES

Susan's story illustrates many of the ways in which secrets operate in therapy. Secrets serve a variety of psychological functions and introduce both a patient and a therapist to important historical issues. Moreover, Susan's case also highlights the role of the therapeutic alliance in the revelation of impulsive theft and gives us further insights into this fascinating disorder. Although Susan's journey is far from over, she has accomplished a great deal in her first four years of serious treatment.

For a variety of reasons, Susan's story is significant.

Certainly, it represents a history replete with boundary violations, childhood traumas, sexual themes, and betrayals of trust.

At first, Susan fought to keep repressed or secret
her increasing awareness of violent and sexual themes.
When thoughts of possible sexual abuse began surfacing,
she consciously suppressed images and thoughts. She felt
uncomfortable discussing her family's history of multiple
boundary violations, both past and present. She also suppressed images of her dreams, associations, choice of
words, secrecy, dissociation, and her lack of memory of the
first fourteen years of her life. She also concealed various
physiological responses manifested during the therapy.

Additionally, Susan's distrust of men, her inability to
engage in intimate relationships, and increasingly disturbing
conscious images of her father and his disruptive, out-of-
control behavior caused her great anxiety. However, despite
her desire to shut down and ignore these powerful issues, she
did finally reveal inappropriate sexual behavior by her father
and severe physical abuse from her cousin.

Susan's constellation of signs and symbols is far
reaching. Anxiety, mood swings, depressions, and suicidal
ideation are all included. Social isolation, an inability to
achieve intimacy, and chronic appetite disturbance are also
prominent. Her therapy revealed many important themes,
some of which may be instrumental in the development of
kleptomania. Typical of kleptomaniacs, the majority of
Susan's signs and symptoms predated the development of her
stealing behavior.

Ultimately, Susan's revelations, whether conscious or
unconscious, were unpleasant and experienced as unwelcome
intrusions. These acts of disclosure bring to mind the "forced

silence" dimension of trauma—in which the child is told never to divulge her shared secret with anyone for fear of severe punishment. For Susan, both secrecy and revelation were associated with great risk and anxiety. She felt compelled to remain silent.

Let's examine another sufferer's experiences in order to formulate some cohesive ideas about kleptomania's role in response to great turmoil.

CHAPTER 14

"I Steal Because I'm Bad"

"Why would you want to help someone who steals?"
– Paula

Paula was twenty-six and an inpatient in a psychiatric unit when she learned of my interest in kleptomania. After reading some materials I had given her, she agreed to be interviewed. Plagued with a variety of severe psychiatric symptoms since she was a child, she had struggled with ongoing issues of self-loathing and self-hatred. She had already been in psychotherapy for several years and had come to understand quite a bit about herself. Because she could not understand why she stole, Paula, like others with stealing behaviors, was completely bewildered. While the thefts made her feel better for a short period of time, they ultimately made her feel worse. Despite her extreme guilt and remorse, she was unable to cease this seemingly senseless behavior.

Despite the fact that she had engaged in such behavior since she was eight, Paula had never spoken to anyone about her stealing. She began by expressing her gratitude for being given the opportunity to speak openly:

"It is important to me. I have never spoken to anyone before about this, because it is so embarrassing. I feel as though people are watching me to see if I take anything on the unit. It makes me feel like a bad person. I do not associate my behavior with any disorder. I am just a bad person. Bad people do this, so I must be bad. I am forever trying to convince my therapist that I do not have a conscience, and that I am just a bad person.

"Since I was born, I guess I have a history of not thinking very much of myself. It goes back a long time. I do not have many memories of my childhood, but the things I do remember are not good. I know that I saw my first psychiatrist when I was eight. From what I have been told, I was the perfect child. I walked and talked at the right ages. I did not cry. I amused myself and spent a lot of time by myself. I did not fuss or have temper tantrums. They said that, for hours, I would sit and put blocks in a bucket.

"My earliest memory was when I was in third grade. My family had just moved from Washington. I was sick, and I ended up in the hospital. No one believed I was sick. I recently got my medical records, and I had some kind of bladder infection and other problems down there that today would signify abuse. I remembered that the doctors asked me if I 'played doctor' with anyone. I do not remember it very clearly. Somebody thought that maybe there was some kind of inappropriate behavior going on. I have no memory of any kind of trauma or abuse going on at that age.

"I was one of seven children. There were three girls

and four boys, and I was somewhere in the middle. I guess when I was about two my mother attempted suicide. In an attempt to piece all of this together, I recently asked my family who took care of us. I got three different answers, so I do not know if anybody took care of us. I did not know about any of this until I first attempted suicide. My mother then told me she attempted suicide because of postpartum depression, but then I found out that she was having an affair and felt guilty. She was in a state hospital for two months. I was without a mother. She was, and always has been, severely, severely depressed.

"I have no memory from ages two to seven. I was told I had friends in the neighborhood and that we took vacations in Mexico a lot, but I only know what I am told. My parents liked to go dancing, and I know they used to leave us kids home alone with my brother in charge. He is only a couple of years older than me. He would have been only four.

"At age eight, I started stealing. I remember stealing two silver dollars from my uncle's dresser and throwing them on the floor and saying, 'Hey, look what I found.' My parents threatened to call the police on me. The first time I went to see a psychiatrist was after I took the money, and I bought a doll for a girl at school. I remember that my mother could not tolerate me or my behavior at all. She did not like me at all. She called me fat all the time. I was not built like my sisters, but I was probably an appropriate weight for my age. The more my mother called me fat, the more I ate in front of her. I did not know what else to do.

"I used to take people's lunches, too. I wanted some. I would take it and then throw it away. I would not eat it. My mother would not pack us lunch. I remember my sisters and

I stayed up late one night to pack our lunches because we wanted to, and she caught us and there was hell to pay. When I went to take someone's lunch, I was feeling needy. I wanted to be like everyone else. I wanted to feel normal. I felt if I took their lunch, that maybe part of them would come with it, and I would be a better person. I did not have to take the lunch as if I had nothing to eat, but I could not stop myself. It happened so quickly. It was never planned. All of a sudden, I was doing it—my heart was racing and it was over. It was terrifying, but after I took something, I felt kind of happy that I did not get caught. Then I would feel terrible, terrible, terrible. I could not sleep, and I would get anxious.

"There must have been something I liked about taking. Maybe I wanted attention. I remember when my grandparents would come over, I would take money from them and it was so obvious. The money was always given back because I would say, 'Oh, look! I found five dollars,' and they would open their wallet and five dollars would be missing. So I gave myself up. The older I got, I did not do that though. I do not know if I took from my siblings. It was an open kind of thing. It was 'What's yours is mine, and what's mine is yours' including clothes, friends, and boyfriends. We shared boyfriends as teenagers. It was horrible. I had a boyfriend for several years, but my parents decided that he was better for one of my sisters. I went away for a weekend, and he spent the weekend at my house with my parents and my sister. They did not like me. I was very different. My mother could not stand the fact that I liked to stay home and read, while my sisters went out on dates. I never drank or went out partying, and it baffled her.

"There was a lot of tension back then. My father

always called my mother 'cold.' There was no physical violence between them—just emotional stuff. They also differed on how to punish me for taking things. I got hit with the belt a few times by my father. It did not help. They would just punish me and send me to my room, which is where I wanted to be anyway. I would read for hours, and I would be by myself. There were many times I said I was never going to talk to these people again, but when you are eight or nine you do not have much choice. I remember once when we were away on vacation, I told everyone that I was going to kill myself and no one listened. When I was about twelve, we went up north. I literally tied myself to the house because I did not want to go home. Nobody took me seriously. They still did not want to admit that there was something wrong.

"I am assuming that, during these years, I was still taking stuff. According to my family, I am a thief beyond belief, beyond all help and hope. I got blamed for everything that was missing.

"When I was twelve-years-old, my brother molested me. I remember it like it was yesterday. I can talk about it because this part of the story I can say without any feeling. My brother chased me upstairs and jumped on the bed and was kissing my breasts. At the time, I did not know what he was doing. My sisters had gone off to the candy store and left me there with my brother. I do not know where my parents were. It continued after that and became actual sex after that. I tried to tell my friends, but nobody would believe me. In the beginning I resisted, but, after awhile, I went with it because I already felt like I was a bad person and this was just one more thing. More badness. My parents were not around a lot, so I had to try to protect my sisters from him.

"I was still stealing. I also was writing letters to myself saying what a bad person I was, and how I should be kicked out of school. People found the letters and finally figured out it was me. I would leave them in my locker and then say, 'Oh! Look what I found in my locker,' to try to make them believe that someone was putting these letters in my locker. Despite this, I still did not get any help. My uncle, who was the gym teacher at the school, did not even tell my parents because my siblings were all very sick physically at one time or another, and he figured that my parents were stressed out enough. I was stealing every day—money, clothes, socks, makeup—all from the locker room. I would take the clothes. I would never wear them. I would just bring them home. I was stealing a lot of lunches. I never—ever!—took from a store.

"We looked like such the perfect family. Appearances were so important. Oh, my goodness. My sisters are very tall and thin and were dressed to kill. You needed to have a boyfriend. I was different. I was an 'A' student and was in the band. I was getting fat. In terms of emotional appearances, no one ever told me to keep my problems to myself, but it was implied. When we moved from Washington, we moved to a town where a lot of the people were related to me, so I had uncles and aunts in the school system, working in the hospital, and in the police department. So it was very important to play the good part. I remember the first time I tried to kill myself. One of my teachers wrote me a letter saying, 'How dare I do this to my family.'

"I would break down in the school hallway and cry, and still people thought that I was just a bad person. When I was fifteen, I put my hand through a window, then cut myself

with a razor blade to make it worse. I was still being molested
by my brother. Also, my parents said that I should not have a
boyfriend because I was so fat and even told my boyfriend
this. I was stealing things from my boyfriend's house at that
time. I used to burn myself with an iron, too. My parents did
not know. They thought that the burns were accidents. I
burned myself on the arms and legs. I cut my face once. I
have scars from cutting that run up my arms. I actually just
burned myself last week.

"When I hurt myself, it is an extreme release of
anxiety. I wait until the tension mounts—but it is impulsive,
like the stealing. I used to keep razor blades with me, just in
case I needed them! Isn't that awful? Both my stealing and
cutting are impulsive. It is a vicious circle. I get tense, I cut
or steal, I feel better, then worse. Then I do it all over again.
The stealing has gotten worse.

"I was not having any other symptoms at that time
except nightmares. Nightmares have always been a part of my
life. I see people molesting me all the time, and I feel them
on me. I had a dream when I was pregnant that someone
killed my dog, and the blood was dripping down the ceiling
onto me and my husband while we were in bed. I wake up as
if someone is touching me.

"When I was a teen, I would try to have sex with my
boyfriend, but I would end up crying and screaming. I feel
anxious talking about my sexuality. I do not know if I ever
had intercourse with my brother or with my boyfriend. I think
I did with my boyfriend, but I just cannot remember. It is too
disturbing to think about. Sex is a very different feeling and
experience for incest survivors. I think that if I had a gun in
my night table, every time I had an orgasm, I would shoot

myself. You feel so horrible. It brings back so many memories and feelings. I want to be intimate with my husband and I initiate it, and then I get all upset. If it feels good, I get really upset.

"About this time, though, I stole something from someone at school and got caught. I told my boyfriend while we were sitting in the car talking. My mother saw me and yelled out the window that I was a slut and to come into the house before the neighbors started talking. The next day, I overdosed and ended up in the hospital. I have been hospitalized almost fifty times. I was in a coma once from an overdose of drugs and alcohol.

"The stealing persisted. When I was sixteen, I took a harmonica from my cousin's house and put it in my suitcase. My family found it. My parents went nuts. It scares me to death. I do not know why I would do something that scares me. It makes me feel so horrible, yet I do it again. I think I wanted to let people know about my stealing back then, but, as I got older and realized what I was doing to my friends and other people, it became very important to keep it a secret.

"After I graduated from high school, I got a job but overdosed and was fired. I took food from the workplace and would buy things for my girlfriends with money I had stolen. Then I moved in with my grandparents who were alcoholics. I was starting to drink a lot and developed bulimia. I was drinking Ipecac and abusing laxatives and was promiscuous as well. I weighed close to two hundred pounds. I will not tell you what I weigh now because I like to keep it a secret. It was time of my life that I felt very ashamed about. My grandfather recently died. I feel very sad about that. It was a big loss for me. I think he loved me very much.

"At eighteen, I moved into a halfway house for mentally ill people. Back then, I was called a 'borderline.' I hated that phrase. During those years, I was *in* the hospital more than *out*. I was hurting myself a lot and was manipulative. If I was being restrained, the staff used to say, 'She's just a borderline.' It is the same thing my parents used to do—that I was just doing this because I had nothing better to do.

"I was at the halfway house because my parents did not want me at home. I worked and paid for my own room and board, but I was molested by the social worker there. He invited me to his house. He was nice to me and older and nice looking. He had told me that the reason he let me into the halfway house was because I needed attention, and that was what he was giving me.

"I was drinking a lot, bulimic, and hurting myself, but I was not stealing. Probably I did not need to because I was doing all these other things.

"I met my husband when I was a little older. We had a baby, which was very stressful. My husband did not want a lot to do with her, and I took care of her alone for the first three months. I was up all night and finally had a breakdown. I tried to make things perfect. I started hallucinating. I was psychotic—seeing bugs and hearing voices. I could not sleep. I was crying a lot. I was not stealing, though. I was hospitalized.

"I also have a terrible anxiety problem. I worry all the time. I worry that the house will catch on fire or carbon monoxide will get us. I am fearful that people do not like me, and I get anxious when someone watches me. I cannot relax.

"I am afraid to throw away things I steal because I am afraid they will trace my garbage, and I will get caught. I have a box upstairs with things in it—makeup, combs, and brushes that I have never used. I am afraid that, if I die, they will find all the stuff. If I throw stuff out, I double bag it.

"I do not think about it before I take. If I see something, I automatically go for it without thinking. I can prevent myself from stealing. The guilt prevents me sometimes. I recently stopped myself from stealing from a friend. I really needed to have it. I took it, but put it back. I was shaking. Typically, my heart palpitates, and I sweat when I steal. I left feeling good that day, though.

"If I am not doing it, I am not thinking about it. I do not plan it at all. I do not walk around thinking about it at all.

"Stealing changes my focus. Maybe I am thinking about what my brother did or my anger toward my mother. It gives me something else to think about for a little while. It makes me feel powerful and in control. Then I feel terrible. Like a drug, like cutting. It is relieving and then painful. I do not think I am addicted to stealing any more than I feel I am addicted to hurting myself.

"I feel guilty every time someone steals something. Somehow, I feel like I infected them with myself. It reminds me of what I have done. I feel like I am a nut. I steal, and I have weird thoughts. I see dead bodies on the shelves in the grocery store.

"Lately, if I go a week without stealing anything, I feel so much better about myself. I took a barrette from my friend last summer. It is in my closet. I do not use it. I also took some magazines and threw them in my bag. I put them in my bathroom. She came over and saw them, with her name on them. I denied it at first, but then told her I did it. She will not talk to me now. I have another friend who will not talk to me, either. With these experiences, you would think that I would not do this anymore because I do not want to lose any friends.

"I feel depressed talking about it. We went way back to my childhood and my grandfather dying and the stealing and losing my friends. The more people like me, the more I feel a need to steal. I cannot figure out why they like me, so I put a stop to the friendship. It is not a very happy topic. It is like a gateway to all my misery.

ONGOING THEMES

Like other people suffering from kleptomania who have told their stories, Paula was cautious when speaking about her habits and behaviors. Her tale is fraught with disturbingly common themes, including boundary violations, traumatic experiences, lifetime depression, anxiety, and self-destructive behaviors. She seemingly has little to gain from stealing—and a lot to lose. She has lost the trust of her family and has been forced to sever friendships because of her stealing and self-hatred. However, her self-hatred started long before her theft. Paula also has a long history of psychosis, as characterized by hallucinations, illusions, and paranoid ideation, signs and symptoms that do not exclude a diagnosis of kleptomania.

Although she and her family believe she is little more than a common thief, her powerful connection to the topic and losses due to stealing are reminders that the differences between kleptomania and ordinary theft for material gain are clear.

Paula's story is a bit unusual in that her kleptomania began at an early age. However, it is not surprising that part of her motivation, albeit unconscious, was to punish and isolate herself from the rest of humanity. Her behavior, which she recognized as destructive, has contributed strongly to her perception of herself as a bad person. The vicious cycle of depression, anxiety, guilt, and need leading to stealing behavior is obvious.

CHAPTER 15

Complex Life Stories

"Let me use the ugliest and most honest words to describe what I sometimes do, and what I loathe myself for."
— Beth

Like fingerprints or snowflakes, no two patients suffering from mental illness are ever identical. While two individuals may seem alike clinically, the complexity of their life circumstances sets them apart from each other in innumerable ways. Although all kleptomaniacs steal, they do so for a variety of reasons.

The burst of emotion accompanying patient disclosures of kleptomania is significant—it appears to accompany an array of unpleasant memories and associations. Despite the temporary relief derived from stealing, people suffering from kleptomania do not look back upon their thefts with pleasant associations or fond memories: their few moments of solitude and peace are obtained at a painful price. Kleptomania represents the tip of the clinical iceberg. A person suffering from kleptomania has a long, complex life story to tell.

RISK FACTORS AND ASSOCIATED PROBLEMS

Who is at risk to develop kleptomania? What are the commonalities that accompany or lead to it? Analysis of case reports, discussions with patients, and review of the literature suggest that a variety of signs and symptoms may be present before, during, and after the development of kleptomania. These may predate the development of kleptomania and accompany kleptomaniacs throughout their lives:

- Profound sadness and depression or irritability
- Anxiety
- Mood swings
- Imagined or real loneliness or isolation
- Present or past struggles with addictions
- Suicidal feelings or behaviors
- Bulimia or other appetite problems
- Tumultuous lives (past or present)
- Lack of an empathetic childhood
- Identity disturbances
- Self-doubt
- Poor self-esteem
- Self-loathing
- Guilt feelings
- A feeling or sense of entitlement to behave in certain ways
- History of losses
- Participation in physically or emotionally self-defeating or destructive behaviors

• Traumatic experiences
• Feelings of emptiness
• Lack of an emotional support system
• Sexual identity issues
• Secrets

Let us examine some of these topics in detail.

DEPRESSION AND ANXIETY REVISITED

We have already discovered that lifelong depression accompanies kleptomania. Up to this point, we have discussed depression in terms of its relationship to sleep and appetite disturbances, sad mood, and lack of energy. In many cases of kleptomania, however, the sadness is so pervasive that it seems to constitute a part of an individual's identity. The depth of depression precludes easy treatment with medication or therapy. Many people cannot find relief from their persistent sadness, or else they experience only brief bursts of good feelings, which, to others, may be viewed as "mood swings."

THE BATTLE BETWEEN RIGHT AND WRONG: A PERSISTENT SENSE OF BADNESS

"I felt filthy."
"I am a sinner."
"I would rather die than tell you certain things."
"I steal because I am bad."
"Why would you want to help someone who steals?"

What crime deserves such self-reproach? While

these kleptomaniacs were uninhibited enough to deprive others of material goods, none did so without remorse and guilt. Issues of morality, sin, guilt, and remorse are persistent, and sufferers carry on an active, conscious and unconscious battle between right and wrong. The need to steal temporarily outweighs the need to be "good" or "proper."

Perhaps no one better relates the story of despair and self-loathing brought about by stealing than Beth. We saw in chapter twelve how she described her focus on tremendous guilt feelings, self-reproach, and remorse, when she said, "Let me use the ugliest and most honest words to describe what I sometimes do, and what I always loathe myself for. Let me use the most brutal, clearest words to try to cut open what infects, so that I cannot kid myself that it is something else."

Beth acknowledges the need to steal, but, because it goes against everything she was taught, she cannot live with herself.

Lara suffers as well. We saw her acknowledgement: "I would steal to make myself feel better." But then she added, "I also felt so very ashamed. On the other hand, I beat myself up emotionally about it because stealing is wrong. I grew up thinking and being taught that stealing was wrong. I am carrying around an extra burden, and I feel I should go to confession."

While patients describe their feelings about theft in terms of guilt and self-reproach, is it necessarily the kleptomania that makes them feel this way? Would patients hate themselves anyway? It was clear in Paula's case that she felt full of "badness" long before she started to steal. Does stealing give people suffering from kleptomania more of an excuse to hate themselves? My sense is that patients have a long history of self-hatred: kleptomania just gives them even more of an excuse to dislike themselves. However, since stealing promotes self-worth and isolation, attempts at both mollification and self-punishment fail.

THE ISSUE OF SEXUALITY

Much of the early literature on kleptomania and sexuality came from psychoanalytic writers, such as Fenichel, who felt that kleptomania could have direct sexual meaning: "A woman of forty who constantly reverted to thievery reported that she was sexually excited whenever she stole, and that she even experienced orgasm at the moment she accomplished her theft. In sexual intercourse she was frigid; while masturbating, she would imagine that she was stealing."

Other early psychiatrists felt that the kleptomaniac was "doing a forbidden thing secretly" and likened the behavior to a sexual act. Wittels observed that stealing was the sex life of the sexually "underdeveloped" kleptomaniac. While much of the traditional literature on sexuality was derived from psychoanalysis, such discussions also take place in nonacademic publications. In a recent *Self* magazine article titled, "Addicted to Stealing," in which I was quoted, the author tells the story of "Kate," who became so sexually aroused while shoplifting that she was able to experience an orgasm by briefly touching her genital area.

Such cases are interesting, but do not represent the majority of people suffering from kleptomania. These cases are noteworthy only because they are the exceptions. Many different people, with a variety of psychological disturbances, may well engage in sexually maladaptive behaviors.

Are issues of sexuality prominently featured in scientific journal articles about kleptomania? For the majority of reported literature cases, no mention was made of sexuality. In those few cases where it was mentioned, individuals admitted to having experiences such as vaginismus, nonarousal, promiscuity alternating with abstinence, and a preoccupation with sterility. Some did report orgasm, or sexual excitement, during theft. Because of a bizarre sexual practice, authors seem to have preferred cases that were unusual or interesting. The reverse may also be true: people with such unusual experiences may have chosen not to report them for fear of being judged, embarrassed, or having to give up one of their secrets.

In my own practice, rather than bizarre orgasmic symptoms, I have discovered sexual conflicts that seem more consistent with other, less concrete issues. Kleptomania does not seem to be about the sex act or orgasms. It is more about issues of identity. Issues of sexuality for the kleptomaniac are far more representative of who they are and what they want or need.

Clearly, no issue of sexuality can be discussed unless it is placed in context. We have seen numerous examples of a variety of people suffering from kleptomania whose sense of who they are is reflected in their behaviors. In Lara's case, she experienced any number of different sexual experiences because she struggled with her sense of identity.

"I would let boys kiss me and touch me," she told me. "I did it because I was looking for love in all the wrong places. I was looking for something to help me feel good about myself, but it made me feel rotten. Just like stealing. I knew it was wrong, but I did it anyway because I knew there was something in my body that someone wanted. I felt rejected by my parents, and I was searching for other experiences to make me feel more whole, more of a person. I have been sexually numb since."

Promiscuous at age nine, out of control sexually while married, struggling with issues of homosexuality, and finally experiencing a sexual "numbness" and abstinence, Lara obviously faced issues that have little to do with the actual physical behavior of kleptomania.

Susan, whose sexual encounters with men were intolerable, preferred other, but equally emotionally risky experiences. For Beth, having an affair while married was significant because it signaled a temporary cessation in stealing. We have seen how Paula described her sexuality in stark terms, saying, "I think that, if I had a gun in my night table every time I had an orgasm, I would shoot myself. You feel so horrible. It brings back so many memories and feelings. I want to be intimate with my husband, and I initiate it and then I get all upset. If it feels good I get really upset."

Kleptomania, with its excitement and risk, likely serves as a transition between mature sexuality and a more primitive, self-gratifying behavior or stance. It may be used with other behaviors as a bridge between a healthy adult and a more infantile person seeking some comfort. The difference between these and older theories is that "stealing is the sex life of the kleptomaniac" does not appear to be constant. It comes and goes as the person either changes for the better or temporarily regresses due to internal or external conflict. It is a fluid system. One sufferer admitted, "Just before I would take something, my body would feel shaky and excited. I would be nervous that I would be caught, but it was a challenge—power, excitement, risk."

Like casual or fearful intercourse, kleptomania is temporarily both biologically exciting and terrifying. The result of both, however, is a quick, potentially hazardous, vicarious thrill that lasts for a very short time and may have an abundance of powerfully devastating consequences.

SELF-MUTILATION AND SELF-DESTRUCTION

People suffering from kleptomania may experience depression, anxiety, mood swings, appetite and identity disturbances, feelings of emptiness and isolation, and a sense that life is not worth living.

Jenny, a thirty-two-year-old medical assistant with a lifelong history of difficult interpersonal relationships, depression, anxiety, and suicidal feelings, acts out her drama in a violent way. She has engaged in repetitive self-mutilation and has cut herself at least twice a week for years. She also engages in a variety of other risky behaviors and has many of the kinds of clinical characteristics common to those suffering from kleptomania. While such cases are generally rare in kleptomania (most kleptomaniacs do not cut or injure themselves), Jenny's story captures a clinical element that cannot be ignored: kleptomania's association with self-destructive behavior.

Ultimately, kleptomania itself is a self-destructive, perhaps even self-abusive, behavior. While the "rush" of theft may be present, it is short-lived and comes at a considerable price. We have seen what it can do to an already poor self-image, not to mention the misery of arrest and accompanying humiliation. Since many of the characteristics of those who cut themselves and those with kleptomania are similar, is kleptomania a symbolic form of self-mutilation? We have heard Paula tell us: "I have scars from cutting that run up my arms. I actually just burned myself last week. When I hurt myself, it is an extreme release of anxiety. I wait until the tension mounts, but it is impulsive, like the stealing. I used to keep razor blades with me, just in case I needed them! Isn't that awful? Both my stealing and cutting are impulsive. It is a vicious circle. I get tense, and I cut or steal. I feel better, then worse, and then I do it all over again."

Patients who cut themselves do so for a variety of reasons. Usually, they are prone to overwhelming feelings of shame, guilt, and self-hatred. Those who engage in such behavior seem to be looking for ways to relieve tension and anxiety, and generally suffer from lifelong depression and have interpersonal difficulties. In cutting themselves, they are looking for ways to numb themselves from psychic pain.

Many patients who injure themselves in this way often feel no pain, or they may even feel elation or have pleasant feelings. Some feel compelled to cut themselves to dissipate mounting feelings of tension and anxiety. After completing the act and experiencing a quick fix of sorts, they tend to develop pain and regret. The cycle of self-hatred then continues, contributing to the already downward spiral of self-contempt and loathing.

In a search for relief, cutting may take on a life of its own—patients may find the behavior becomes habit-forming and virtually impossible to cease.

If the word "stealing" could be substituted for "cutting" in Paula's description, her account could just as easily hold true for kleptomania. There seems to be a parallel between the self-mutilation seen in those who cut (or overdose, or burn, for example) and those who steal.

Other clinical researchers have noticed a relationship between impulse disorders and self-mutilation. In discussing those patients (not necessarily kleptomaniacs) who may use actual self-mutilation, Favazza notes that "Patients with the repetitive self-mutilation syndrome demonstrate a pattern of uncontrolled, repetitive self-harm in response to disturbing psychological symptoms or environmental events. They are captive to their preoccupation with their acts of self-harm, experience cravings (just as pathological gamblers do if they are unable to gamble), and may assume an identity as a cutter."

Remember Beth's conscious conflict: "When I become overwhelmed by depression, I cannot focus, and I cannot process fast enough. I need quiet and time alone. Then I might steal something. Sometimes I resist, but, at this point, the thought comes to mind much too often."

Beth, like others suffering from kleptomania, clearly finds stealing to be painful and self-injurious. But, at the same time, she uses it to treat her depression. Like Favazza's example, she is captive to the preoccupation.

ROTATING IMPULSES: THE SCOURGE OF ADDICTION

An individual does not need to cut or burn him or herself to be a kleptomaniac. In some instances, though, destructive impulses tend to be interchangeable. For some patients, kleptomania appears to be episodic and not constant. Lara, as we have seen, used both cutting and stealing for self-relief and described her behavior: "I cut myself. I used to cut myself a lot. It would take the other pain away. It would give me a sense of peace and relief. It was a good kind of pain, a better pain than what I was going through inside. It was a distraction."

Lara agreed that cutting was like stealing. The powerful emotional state and short-term relief are similar in both behaviors. At one point, Paula wondered why she *was not* stealing. She then considered that she was bulimic (and tried drinking), so she did not "need" the stealing behavior. The other behaviors were "getting the job done" for her. In both stealing and self-mutilation, patients are plagued by the same cycle of self-reproach. Like cutting, stealing can clearly be habit-forming. In describing her difficulties, Lara likened her thievery and other impulses to an addiction: "Even back then, I guess I was going from one addiction to the next. I think I have been substituting one addictive behavior for another. When one behavior did not give me what I needed, I would move on to the next."

Clinicians have noted a relationship between kleptomania and other impulsive behaviors. In discussing the case of a twenty-six-year-old female with a history of kleptomania, bulimia, and compulsive shopping, Schwartz comments that: "Kleptomania may be replaced by bulimia, wrist-cutting, or drug abuse."

In a personal communication, Favazza states that he has encountered an interesting group of patients "in whom cutting and burning seem to develop a life of their own. These patients harm themselves repetitively and often develop an eating disorder and/or episodic alcohol abuse and/or kleptomania."

In my experience, many of the patients suffering from kleptomania may also be plagued by rotating addictive self-destructive behaviors, including sexual acting out, drug and alcohol abuse, hospital addiction, eating disorders, and self-mutilation. Such behaviors tend to take on a life of their own. Sufferers may be so busy going from one behavior to the next and recovering from the negative consequences of their actions, that they have little time for anything else. Their identities become dependent on these behaviors.

All these characteristics contribute to both the pain of stealing as well as the lure or seduction of crime—the false hope or belief that developmental issues can be resolved through maladaptive behavior. Kleptomania and other "replacement behaviors" are impulses so strong that patients place themselves at considerable risk because they are unable to generate their own internal happiness. Ultimately, such behaviors backfire because they make patients feel powerless and out of control.

With few exceptions, kleptomania appears to begin only after a person's personality style and characteristics have been formed. Usually it begins during the person's twenties, and only after he or she has enjoyed stealing as a youth. The resulting enjoyable feeling provides the person with the template or foundation upon which the learned behavior of kleptomania is formed. The initial theft was *exciting*—a feeling almost serendipitous to the original intent of the theft. This interesting feeling unconsciously "hooked" the sufferer and fulfilled whatever function stealing served for them.

The development of kleptomania may be one of the last behavioral manifestations, or the final common pathway, in a person with lifelong issues of emptiness and desperation. For the average sufferer, kleptomania seems to develop after other equally disturbing life problems or maladaptive behaviors have begun. Kleptomania drains its sufferers of their dignity and self-respect. It prevents them from ever feeling good about themselves for more than several minutes at a time and leaves them with an insidious, ongoing moral confusion.

Kleptomania may, however, be merely the vehicle that gives structure and meaning to suffering and conflict—conflict that predates the development of a stealing problem.

CHAPTER 16

Does It Make
Any Sense?

*"Self-destructive activities are [were] not primarily related
to conflict, guilt, and superego pressure, but to more primitive behavior patterns originating in painful encounters with
hostile caretakers during the first years of life."*
            – Simpson and Porter

Kleptomania represents, among other things, a cycle
of attempted gratification followed by a profound sense of
badness and sadness. The end result is self-hatred.
Kleptomania seems to be a self-abusive, self-destructive
behavior, similar to self-mutilation. Simpson and Porter feel
that self-destructive behavior may be rooted during early
childhood development.

Empathic Failures: An Eternity of Deprivation, Emptiness and Loss

Depression, anxiety, sexuality, self-abuse, addictions,

and similar issues appear to be related to issues of identity. From what are these identity issues derived? What is their most significant common denominator? It is probably the complex issue of *loss*. We have all experienced losses— failures, death of loved ones, and the like. But most of us never develop kleptomania. So what is the relationship between *loss* and *stealing*?

Empathy, the ability of one person to feel and to respond to what another person feels, is central to the development of a healthy sense of self. Without such positive empathic experiences in childhood—from parents or care- givers, for example—a child can develop into an untrusting adult who will be constantly searching for love. Without trust, adults can be developmentally blunted, consistently searching for a firm sense of where they fit into the world. The result is identity confusion, self-hatred, fear, distrust, a sense of emptiness, and a deep sense of loss.

What kind of concrete examples of empathic failures have we seen? For Lara, her parents' frequent absences, their lack of limits, and their lack of concern for her physical and emotional well-being all reveal a profound deficit in empathy and parenting. Lara was left to care for herself and her sib- lings. *Her* complaints, fears, and concerns were never con- sidered. For Susan, we recognize empathic failure in her physically tumultuous childhood, with frequent beatings and lack of parental intervention. For Beth, it was a family which was strict, rigid, and unforgiving. And Paula's family was unfeeling and uncaring; not only did they set poor boundaries, but they failed to believe her complaints and did not protect her from abuse.

Those suffering from kleptomania may have been the products of tumultuous childhoods and also may have been rejected by important role models. Most seemed to have suffered in relative silence, and some were told to keep their problems and those of the family to themselves. Appearances were extremely important. This relative lack of strong parental guidance and support in the face of adversity is a form of deprivation and loss. How is this important? It seems that the relationship between loss and kleptomania comes not so much from a present or current loss (which may, of course, begin the cycle of theft again) but rather from a multitude of losses over many years.

What are some of the other attitudes and behaviors that may develop as a result of these failures? For many, the resultant tumult of childhood has left them with a deep sense of identity confusion. Feelings of fragmentation and desperation can lead to self-destructive measures—measures, paradoxically, designed to make themselves feel whole again.

How do some people soothe themselves in an environment lacking in support? Stealing seems to provide a portion with forbidden, exciting, and soothing indulgences. In Paula's case, the thefts also provided continuity from her early punitive home life; she, in turn, learned to punish herself. Thus, it seems reasonable to assume that *early losses* are, in some way, related to the development of kleptomania.

While early—or original—losses can lead to profound sadness and depression as well as a multitude of other problems, patients often unconsciously only experience loss in adulthood as original loss. Thus, troubled marriages, being fired or reprimanded at work, or being slighted may all create intense feelings. Since few positive experiences are available to fall back on, patients with unpleasant early life experiences may react poorly to current disruptions in their lives. It is this episodic reminder in the present that perpetuates the cycle of despair. How are these losses experienced? In an attempt to compensate, how do patients react to or against the symbolic representations of the hostility and loss of childhood? How do they mourn the loss of childhood?

MOURNING THE LOSS: WHAT IS IN IT FOR ME?

Earlier, we touched upon some of the "benefits" derived from stealing. We know, for example, that stealing can be an anxiety-relieving behavior and can also function as an antidepressant. Let us explore these mechanisms, and what they mean in greater detail.

When people lose something important—a car, a friend, or money, for example—they understandably become upset. What happens, though, when the loss is of monumental emotional importance—such as a loss of parental love, for example? Kleptomania may well be a signal denoting that a person is in a chronic state of mourning for a real or perceived loss. Such people are, in effect, "grieving." What is gained by stealing? Stealing has a variety of benefits:

- *It results in feeling better emotionally.*
- *It is exciting.*
- *It creates a feeling of specialness.*
- *It fosters feelings of entitlement.*
- *It provides relief, pleasure, or gratification.*
- *It promotes feelings of "getting away with something."*
- *It promotes feelings of power or control.*
- *It moderates, adjusts, or controls anxiety or depressive states.*

When something is taken away, it is only human to want to get something back in return. Kleptomaniacs seem to trade in feelings or affective states noted in the list, designed to "compensate" the patient for loss and deprivation. After all, who wouldn't want to feel powerful, in control, and special in the face of loss? Unfortunately, however, stealing represents a compromise. Stealing also:

• *Results in ultimately feeling worse.*
• *Is dangerous or risk-taking.*
• *Serves as self-punishment.*
• *Is self-defeating.*

Ultimately such behaviors do end up being self-defeating and self-abusive.

To use an analogy, when a foreign object, like a splinter, is introduced into the human body, special blood cells in the body attempt to destroy the object. Actually, the body's response is often injurious: the cellular response causes swelling, pain, and fever. Like a foreign body that will not go away, severe loss and deprivation may become permanently imbedded. Kleptomania represents a desire to be helpful, but often makes things worse.

FULFILLING PRIMITIVE NEEDS: A LINK TO THE PAST

Stealing's positive and negative results detail a broad variety of signs, symptoms, feelings, and thoughts. Are they special in some way? Are they unique to kleptomania? While they broaden our understanding of kleptomania, these signs, symptoms, feelings, and thoughts exist elsewhere—

in patients who have either been traumatized or have experienced seemingly endless emotional insults or losses over the course of a lifetime.

Could stealing be related to trauma? I have certainly noticed many clinical similarities.

It is possible that stealing actually may recreate both the excitement (self-soothing, "specialness") and the shame (guilt, rage, and remorse) experienced by those trying to master early traumatic experiences. Such contrasting feelings are common to both kleptomania and early traumatic experiences. Impulsive behaviors may well be rooted in or derived from a desperate emptiness, which the act of stealing, cutting, or other impulsive behaviors are "intended" to fill.

How can we, who attempt to treat sufferers, explain the apparent "addictive" and physiological effects of stealing and connect them to a psychological model? It is quite common for patients to discuss the *physically arousing response* elicited by the powerful attraction to stealing. Is there a physiological contingent to this sort of theft? What is the physiological counterpart to the emotional drive? What is there about stealing that makes it so "irresistible?" Why does the body seem to "take over" when the mind says "no" to a behavior that appears to make so little sense?

MIND OVER MATTER: BIOLOGICAL SPECULATIONS

Psychiatrists and others in the mental health professions have known for a long time that the body and mind work together both in causing and solving difficult problems. The "fight or flight" response, which occurs when an individual is faced with a dangerous situation, is a good example of this complex interaction. Kleptomania also appears to involve physiology and emotion. How can we create a hypothetical model to help explain the relationship between the two?

Stealing appears to elicit an autonomic nervous system response. Such a response might include, among other things, sweating, rapid heart beat or palpitations, nervousness, excitement, and anxiety—many of the sensations described by those suffering from kleptomania. In addition, a response to theft may include relief of anxiety, pleasure, or gratification.

Traumas, losses, and deprivations can be duplicated by people on many related planes. The body and mind can respond to a broad array of abuses—present and past—on many different levels: behavioral, emotional, physiological, and neuroendocrinological. Those who respond to traumas are often in a state of physiological *hyperarousal*: the *volume*, so to speak, of their many biological and emotional systems is on high and ready to respond to a perceived hostile environment. However, being that "ready" to respond to abuse is costly, because it interferes with the ability to make rational decisions.

Sufferers who have had severely stressful, traumatic experiences will, in response to subsequent stresses, experience large increases in two bodily substances: *endogenous opiates* and *catecholamines*.

While they may have other functions, endogenous opiates, like endorphins, are produced in the brain and released into the blood stream when pain is experienced. Like an opiate, the substances offer relief.

Catecholamines, on the other hand, are substances responsible for the "fight or flight" reaction. They cause the "adrenaline" rush that people experience in times of stress or excitement.

When trauma patients reexperience stress or trauma, their bodies react with a greater release of these substances than the bodies of people who have a less severe life history. This extra release provides the patient with a variety of feelings, including relief. Sufferers with histories of trauma who respond to stress in this fashion may attempt to terminate this hyperarousal by exposing themselves to situations that may result in further release of these soothing and stimulating substances. These situations might include addictive behaviors such as compulsive reexposure to situations that in some way remind them of the trauma—abusive relationships, for example.

Hypothetically, it is possible that, in an attempt to soothe themselves, treat their sadness, and diminish their anxiety, kleptomaniacs steal in order to "stimulate" the release of these substances. The stealing seen in kleptomania may be the mechanism by which attempts are made to modulate or control depression or anxiety states and gain relief from a chronic state of hyperarousal.

Stealing as Trauma: The Endless Cycle of Despair and Relief

Lara's and Paula's memories of their sexual traumas, emotional insults, losses, and deprivations may be *reawakened* by any number of things, such as rocky relationships or rejections. However, psychologically speaking, stealing itself could be a symbolic representation of a past trauma. Alternatively, in an attempt to "master" feelings of despair, the kleptomaniac becomes more like an *aggressor*. As we have seen, kleptomania is often associated with feelings of omnipotence, "specialness," entitlement, fearful or painful pleasure, guilt, shame, disgust, fear of discovery, and secretiveness—all characteristics of a child's emotional response to a trusted adult's abuse.

People who have been traumatized and employ a variety of adaptive behaviors ultimately perpetuate chronic feelings of helplessness—a sense of being "bad" and a loss of control. These feelings and behaviors can lead to great social and personal suffering as can be found in kleptomania. The kleptomaniac's behavior ultimately perpetuates the endless cycle of despair and relief.

However, in using sexual trauma as an example, it is important to note that kleptomania does not necessarily imply a history of such trauma or abuse. The development of kleptomania may be the result of an accumulation of misery spread over many years and not necessarily the result of one or two specific incidences. Additionally, while it seems that many traumatized people may steal, not all who steal have been *sexually* traumatized or abused. Rather, with increasingly severe life experiences, which may include sexual trauma, the chances of developing kleptomania may be increased. Because they are ever searching for ways to feel whole and for ways to "master" their feelings and experiences, kleptomania sufferers may be the most vulnerable.

WHY NOT JUMP OUT OF AN AIRPLANE?

For many kleptomaniacs, the thrill of theft and the rush it elicits are the primary conscious reasons for stealing. By eliminating the feelings of despair, misery, and depression, sufferers are able to achieve a temporary peace of mind.

Yet the powerful physiology of the illness—the body's response to stealing—can easily be duplicated elsewhere. So why steal? Why not just parachute out of an airplane or climb a mountain?

When a kleptomaniac takes risks and steals, the individual is actually doing far more than trying to catch a vicarious thrill. Kleptomania is more than a behavior. It is a psychological and physiological statement, a tip-off or red flag, a powerful affect, and a response to a hostile world. For some people, kleptomania may represent one of many *interchangeable* behavioral self-destructive behaviors—eating disorders, using drugs, or drinking, for example. Many of these problems are likely primitive, basic mechanisms and reflect a *mandate*, but also a *compromise*, issued by the person's unconscious self. It is not clear how the mind decides which coping mechanism to use, but *symbols* appear to play a large part. Our own questionable habits, quirks, or behaviors may also be the results of a kind of sliding scale of pathology based on the sum total of all of our experiences. The results of this process prompt us to do things we might ordinarily not do and often are simply translated into a *symbolic* gesture. One can express hostility in many ways—stealing is one way, murder is another.

For the person suffering from kleptomania, stealing, on top of whatever else it may represent, may symbolize one of the most basic and primitive mechanisms of obtaining a much-needed object quickly. Like a child fighting over a desired object, the kleptomaniac steals, in part, to obtain or possess *potency* and *strength*.

Because it signals the individual's ability to modulate affective states by slipping or regressing to a *transient primitive state* to fulfill psychological and emotional needs, kleptomania is truly a remarkable behavior. Stealing is the avenue through which the body and mind reach down to their most primitive, basic, but adaptive depths. The act of theft, with all its psychological and physiological aspects, is a *"life raft"* to escape going down with a sinking ship. At the same time, the process slowly pokes holes in the life raft, causing it to slowly and steadily sink anyway.

CHAPTER 17

Why Treatments Fail

Unfortunately, as I've said, kleptomania is rarely the only important issue in the lives of patients. For most, depression, anxiety, identity issues, and other emotionally painful issues or conditions frequently accompany stealing behaviors. Let us look at some problems in treating the person who suffers from kleptomania.

RESISTANCE: IMPEDIMENTS TO TREATMENT

We have likened the body's and mind's response to kleptomania to a foreign body's invasion. Kleptomania tries to be helpful but often makes things worse. Why must treatment be so complex? If stealing is ultimately injurious, can't we just remove the "sliver"—give the kleptomaniac a pill? Or fix the depression? Mending, fixing, curing—if it were that simple, patients would flock to treatment. What limits treatment success? Some of the issues complicating treatment, issues that must be understood and overcome if treatment is to succeed are the following:

Initiation: Kleptomania may begin at age twenty. On average though, the disorder is not detected until the patient is thirty-five. That means that stealing has gone largely unchecked for fifteen years. Many forms of emotional difficulties become more difficult to treat the longer they are untreated. In general, patients who are not exposed to intervention early find it increasingly difficult to engage in treatment.

Presentation: Although Susan was engaged in treatment for her depression, anxiety, and social isolation, she was unwilling to disclose her secret of stealing for many years. As with difficulties in initiating treatment, many patients who do eventually enter treatment do not disclose their stealing behavior, or if they do, wait too long. There are many reasons for this—identity preservation and symptom relief, for example. Since so many other things are going wrong in their lives, they may not feel that kleptomania is a priority. Patients may focus on what they see as more acute issues, such as suicidal feelings, family or work crises, and relationship issues.

Recognition: Through no fault of their own, clinicians are often unable to detect secret illnesses, especially if the patient does not allude to them. Therapy may continue, with the emphasis on other issues, or it may be terminated by the patient or therapist citing a "lack of progress." Another problem in a camouflaged disorder such as kleptomania is that most managed-care companies do not provide for lengthy therapy, choosing instead to limit sessions or use them for a focused "piece of work."

Ambivalence: We have seen all the reasons why, even when their kleptomania is discussed in the therapeutic setting, sufferers may be unwilling to consent to treatment.

Mistreatment: In some ways, clinicians are at least partially responsible for the lack of effective treatment of their patients. Often they hope that, if they treat the depression, the signs and symptoms of kleptomania will dissipate. Medication aimed at treating depression is only partially helpful, if at all in treating the disorder.

Another important therapeutic issue is related to the relative scarcity of data available to clinicians who try to treat patients with kleptomania. Few good treatment options exist and long-term studies tracking outcomes are sparse. Clinicians may also be fearful of "symptom substitution," the belief that the removal of one undesirable symptom will lead to the creation of another.

Since no two patients will have the same character structure and may steal for different reasons, a treatment plan must be molded to address each sufferer's specific needs.

Patient Deception: Kleptomania is a powerful drive. Although they want to stop stealing, patients understandably are desperate to maintain their relative health. It is not uncommon for patients to be deceptive about the level and intensity of stealing. This makes for difficult assessment of treatment progress. Full disclosure of *all* stealing episodes is a necessity if treatment is to succeed.

Lack of a Solid Therapeutic Alliance: While there are exceptions, most kleptomaniacs approach treatment cautiously and without great trust in the process—not because they have little faith in the therapeutic process or therapist, but because they have difficulty trusting the world in general. A therapeutic "alliance," regardless of the nature of treatment, is a prerequisite for success. Since, according to Gutheil and

Havens, it allows the healthier part of an emotionally compromised patient to work effectively with the therapist, the alliance can be used to great advantage in the therapeutic process. This must be developed for any important work on the problem to occur.

Poorly Defined Goals: Patients must decide whether or not to risk the consequences of terminating their behavior versus the fears and pains associated with continuing therapy.

Patient Pool: Another possibly confounding treatment factor is related to patient selection. It is possible that patients who *do* present themselves for treatment are the toughest to treat. Many patients who show up for treatment have been referred by the courts. It is possible that these patients represent a more treatment-resistant group.

Character: We have seen how kleptomania seems to be imbedded or ingrained in character and how it seems to form part of the personality of the person who is afflicted. Treating character and identity is very difficult. It takes more than a pill. Often the clinical picture is simply too complex to be just "treatable." The good news, however, is that there are treatments.

CHAPTER 18

Treating Kleptomania

With no specific treatment protocol, no magic pill, or surgery for sufferers of kleptomania, is there hope? Can there be effective treatment? Very definitely *yes*. Patients *do* get better and do so in more ways than one.

While there are different approaches, most treatments fall into one of five categories—shopping avoidance, behavioral, psychotherapy, medication, and combination treatment.

BEHAVIORAL TREATMENTS

Behavioral "treatments" are universal and common. In fact, we all use them—in principle. For example, if a child is given a gold star every time she cleans her room, she'll theoretically be less inclined to have a messy room and more inclined to seek reward for continuation of her good behavior. On the other hand, if a parent spanks a child enough, or threatens to spank, a child will theoretically stop

engaging in the behavior the spanking was meant to stop—
he is being punished for bad behavior. Sometimes the threat
takes on a life of its own. The child might simply *imagine*
being spanked which might, in itself, be enough to dissuade
him from engaging in the behavior—"Gee, if I do this, I'm
going to be punished, so maybe it would be best if I didn't do
it." As strange as it sounds, like the threat of a "spanking,"
most behavioral treatment for kleptomania focuses on the
punishment of impulsive thoughts or behaviors.

Behavioral therapy seeks to alter a lone behavior
through the use of a variety of different methods. Using the
principles of relaxation and suggestion, patients are actually
"taught" to do, or not do, a given behavior. Sound confusing?
Well, like a teacher, the therapist or counselor (usually a psy-
chologist) helps the patient learn. Unlike a conventional
teacher however, the therapist "teaches" the patient how *not
to* engage in a detrimental activity or even how to "unlearn"
a potentially damaging set of behaviors. Sometimes the
"teaching" involves reward. In other words, a positive
behavior might be rewarded. Conversely, depending on the
type of therapy, "bad" behavior might be punished.

It's interesting to note that unlike traditional psychotherapy, where reasons are important, behavioral therapists are not particularly concerned with why a patient is
doing one thing or another. The aim is simply to extinguish
the behavior. Listed below are some of the more common
types of these so-called behavioral techniques.

Aversive Behavioral Treatment: This particular
form of behavioral modification therapy pairs an actual (not
imagined) adverse consequence of stealing with the desire to
steal. Does it work? One researcher, Carolin Keutzer, treated

a twenty-five-year-old woman with a lengthy history of stealing, depression, impaired sexual judgment, and arrests. In response to an impulse to steal, the patient was instructed to hold her breath until moderate discomfort emerged. Using this self-administered breath holding to rid her patient of the desire to steal, Keutzer reported few stealing episodes at a ten-week follow-up. Of course, the efficacy of this treatment was greatly dependent on the patient's willingness to divulge stealing impulse and her dedication to full disclosure of stealing episodes. It's unclear whether the patient remained "stealing free" after that time period.

Aversive treatments can encompass every imaginable form of "punishment." In another case a patient was asked to snap a rubber band against her wrist every time she inched closer to an object she wanted to take. My sense is that these forms of "treatment" have, at best, marginal results and I don't advocate them. Why? Well, for one thing, there aren't any long-term follow-up studies on the effectiveness of these treatments. The other reason is that patients suffering from kleptomania already have enough pain in their lives. Reinforcing further feelings of discomfort seems irrational and gratuitous.

Covert Sensitization: In our prior example, rather than the physical spanking a child might get, sometimes the threat will prevent the child from misbehaving. In covert sensitization, unlike aversive behavioral therapy (where real discomfort is used), fantasy is utilized. Behavioral therapists might teach the kleptomania patient to mentally couple the thought of stealing with an undesirable consequence, such as arrest or humiliation. In covert sensitization therapy, there is one reported case of a man in his mid-twenties with a ten-year history of stealing who was taught to imagine several unpleasant consequences of stealing when he felt the urge or impulse to steal. His therapist explains that "the client would imagine himself in a store having an urge to take an item and then imagine an aversive occurrence, for example getting caught or realizing that the manager was in the rear of the store watching him. . . . Between sessions he was to go into stores, walk up and down the aisles, stop, and imagine someone was watching him from the back of the store."

In this case, the therapist also had the patient imagine a variety of other negative consequences to stealing, such as being apprehended by police, handcuffed and put into a jail cell. After ten months, the patient's stealing episodes diminished markedly. In another case, that of a middle-aged woman, a researcher used images of nausea and vomiting, coupling them with the desire to steal. A nineteen-month follow-up of the treatment revealed only one episode of stealing by the woman, who had stolen daily for almost fifteen years.

Since the treatment of kleptomania is in its infancy, few therapists are experienced in these kinds of treatments for stealing. In addition to this drawback, most patients are so ambivalent that they might not be motivated to enter such treatment even if it could be found. They would rather passively or anonymously accept medication and psychotherapy. As we'll see, psychotherapy and medications have been the mainstays of treatment and it is with these treatment modalities that most psychiatrists are familiar.

When choosing a behaviorally oriented program though, it's important to remember that the sessions can conjure up unpleasant fantasies—fantasies, to be sure, that are designed to be worse, sometimes more horrifying, than the behavior they're meant to prevent. However, since it specifically targets the behavior, behaviorally oriented treatment, I believe, holds great promise. If behavioral treatments are to be used, it's important to remember kleptomania's connection with other issues. These, too, will eventually need treatment.

PSYCHOTHERAPY

Until recently, psychotherapy was the mainstay of treatment for nearly everyone with any sort of emotional complaint. In cases of psychotherapy and kleptomania reported in older psychoanalytic literature, the primary goal was to "tap" into the patient's unconscious, understand the patient's motivations for certain behaviors, and help the patient change the behavior through talk.

Psychoanalysis is a lengthy process and, regarding kleptomania, has yielded mixed results. Although much of the theoretical groundwork has been provided by this type of therapy, there's little well-organized information regarding the efficacy of psychoanalysis or any of the long-term, insight-oriented psychotherapies in the treatment of kleptomania. Psychodynamic therapists have claimed success by treating kleptomania and other forms of stealing as a symptom of an underlying conflict, but long-term follow-up is lacking.

As we've seen, patients suffering from kleptomania have a multitude of other issues and conflicts that can readily be addressed by psychotherapy. Additionally, since virtually nobody appears before any kind of therapist for treatment of kleptomania, intensive psychotherapy serves as a kind of early warning system—that is, it's usually the only way non-referred kleptomaniacs are discovered. In Susan's case, the therapeutic alliance had to be formed over several years before she felt comfortable even bringing up the subject. Since therapists using psychotherapy treat patients for lengthy periods of time, it is really the only vehicle for gaining this kind of disclosure.

What can psychotherapy really do for people suffering from kleptomania? Well, in Susan's case, it was clearly helpful in a variety of ways. Due to the strength of the therapeutic alliance, her secret history of impulsive theft emerged. Her admission of kleptomania seemed to serve as an important introduction to intimacy issues that had previously gone unmentioned. Meares suggests that secrets "become a coin of intimacy, and the currency of its transactions." He believes that the experience of having and sharing a secret is necessary to intimacy because it requires careful disclosure to a trusted other.

It was clear that Susan was unable to discuss issues of sexuality. In fact, there was no specific mention of her own sexuality prior to the disclosure of kleptomania. By first hinting about and then bringing out her kleptomania, she felt free to reveal other difficult issues in a far less symbolic way. Susan felt reassured with the therapist's nonjudgmental acceptance of her behavior. This, in turn, allowed her to proceed in disclosing her stealing behavior and a deeper issue she'd previously censored—intimacy.

I've treated numerous kleptomania sufferers with psychotherapy, not so much to rid them of kleptomania, but to help them move on in their lives. Remember, kleptomania encompasses a complex set of problems and issues, not the least of which is stealing. Depression, anxiety and interpersonal problems are all included in the spectrum of issues relevant to these people. Do patients always want to discuss their stealing in therapy? You'd think so! In the case of Samantha, one of my patients, she had so many other important issues that kleptomania was really the only exciting part of her life. Sam didn't want to discuss it because she feared it might go away and she'd be left with nothing!

In another case, Bob, one of my patients, was so chronically depressed it was almost impossible to discuss anything other than his need to maintain the basic necessities of life. The use of psychotherapy can be very helpful in Bob's and other cases. Alice, another patient I treated, responded well to clinical interventions and interpretation (a statement made by the therapist that endeavors to link present behaviors or thoughts with the past). She was able to recognize that deprivation in her past had led her to wishes to fill herself up by stealing. For the most part, therapy is very hard work and needs to be done slowly and gently. It can be painful and can refresh a patient's memory of past traumatic events. Sometimes it can backfire. Because she linked therapy with various deprivations and traumas, Carolann, a woman I treated, became suicidal when we started to discuss her history of stealing.

After spending many years treating patients suffering from kleptomania, I feel that psychotherapy shouldn't be the sole treatment of choice to rid someone of stealing. Does this mean that kleptomaniacs shouldn't be involved in psychotherapy? Actually, it means just the opposite. All patients suffering from kleptomania should be engaged in therapy, but not necessarily to cease stealing. Cessation of theft might be a pleasant and desirable benefit, but the real advantage comes when a person with complex problems enters into a long relationship with a caring therapist who can help sort through the numerous inevitable issues and conflicts running the person's life.

BIOLOGICAL THERAPIES

Medications have grabbed the headlines lately. It's rare to pick up a newspaper without reading of at least one medication success or disaster for a whole host of disturbances, disorders or even normal conditions. While new psychotropic medications have given psychiatrists treatment options not available a few years ago, there have been very few convincing reports of full "remissions" in patients suffering from kleptomania. Before we explore the specifics of kleptomania treatment outcomes, let's first take a look at the variety of biological therapies used to treat disorders possibly associated with the kleptomania disorder.

Tricyclic Antidepressants: Up until a few years ago, these medications formed the mainstay of treatment for a variety of disorders including depression, eating disorders, and kleptomania. Included in this category are drugs like Elavil, Pamelor, Tofranil, and Norpramin. These medications differ largely in their different side effects. For the most part, they tend to cause constipation, blurry vision, and dry mouth, and may precipitate cardiac difficulties in older patients or in those younger patients with specific forms of heart disease.

Serotonin Re-Uptake Inhibitors: The so-called "SRI's" or "serotonin re-uptake inhibitors" have revolutionized the way we treat depression, eating disorders, impulsivity, anxiety, and a variety of other ailments. These drugs include Prozac, Paxil, Luvox, and Zoloft. The medications are generally well tolerated, they are safer in case of an overdose, and seem to interact more rapidly with the body and result in quicker relief than older medications. The problem? In some ways, their use has been trivialized. People with various normal complaints and issues are placed on them with hardly a thought. The SRI's are being used with increasing frequency for everything from canine misbehavior to bulimia in humans as well as everything in between.

Mood Stabilizers: Like the SRI's, mood stabilizers have become fashionable lately. Drugs like lithium (traditionally used for manic-depressive illness), Tegretol (an anti-seizure drug) and Depakote (also an antiseizure drug), have been used to combat depression, rage, violence, impulsivity, and mania. Unlike the SRI's, these medications have far more potentially serious side effects, especially in overdose.

Atypical Antidepressants: Some medications, like people, can't be fit into any specific category. These medications—Wellbutrin, Remeron, Effexor, Trazadone, Serzone—are all antidepressants but, because of their chemical or structural composition, aren't easily categorized. Many of them have been used in the treatment of depressive disorders, kleptomania, anxiety, sleeplessness,and even smoking cessation.

Anxiolytics: Antianxiety medications are also quite popular. One such medication, Valium, has unfortunately become part of American pop culture. Other medications that reduce the signs and symptoms of anxiety include Ativan, Klonopin, Serax, and Xanax. These medications can be very helpful when used for brief periods of time. However, they can be sedating and become habit-forming, and they may have other potentially serious side effects. BuSpar, an antianxiety medication unrelated chemically to the others, can be effective in controlling impulsivity and anxiety.

ECT (Shock Therapy): While not a medication, ECT or electroconvulsive therapy, has been effective in the treatment of depression for over fifty years. Unlike its portrayal in *One Flew Over the Cuckoo's Nest*, when administered properly modern ECT is safe, effective, and painless. It is never used for punitive reasons and can be literally life-saving in treating those with severe depression or mania.

The literature is full of anecdotal cases of kleptomania being treated with various agents with mixed results. What about more formal studies? In a larger study of twenty kleptomaniacs, a research team found seven "remissions" and four "partial remissions" in patients who had been treated with a variety of antidepressants, anxiolytics (Klonopin) or mood stabilizers (lithium, Depakote). If kleptomania and depression had a simple, straightforward relationship with each other, why then wasn't the response more spectacular?

In my own practice, I've used a variety of medications not only to treat kleptomania but to try and control other more debilitating symptoms. In most cases, medications were able to help soothe patients and precipitate, at best, temporary cessations in stealing. For example, over the years Lara had taken just about every conceivable medication including most of the antidepressants, antianxiety medications, and mood stabilizers. The result? Episodes of severe depression during which she was unable to muster the energy to steal. Once she started to feel better she took to taking again, in order to maintain her "good" feelings.

What about Susan? Susan had taken a variety of medications to try to alleviate her problems. These included

Xanax for anxiety; Paxil for depression, compulsive behavior, and mood swings; and Trazadone for sleep disturbance. The result? Stealing remissions followed by a return to full-blown stealing.

In Paula's case, her stealing seemed to be perpetual. In fact, not even ECT used only to treat her severe depression and suicidal feelings was powerful enough to stop her episodes of stealing. Ironically, medications and ECT appeared to actually make her feel slightly less guilt-ridden when she stole—little solace.

Since many theories posit that stealing may in itself lift depression, why then did these women and other people steal when they felt better? My theory is because "feeling better" to these patients meant only that they could think more clearly about their unpleasant situations. Most cases, like those which I've discussed, seem to have mixed results, and, at best, remissions followed by more stealing. Are medications helpful? Medications alone may diminish but only rarely completely abolish the impulse to steal. In my experience, use of these medications, while effective in treating associated signs and symptoms of depression and anxiety, haven't done nearly as good a job with kleptomania.

Is this bad? Should all hope be abandoned? Certainly not. The use of medications may be very helpful in the treatment of specific issues like those related to trauma. But more important, the use of medications, like psychotherapy, is a vehicle enabling formerly depressed, anxious or traumatized patients to work on their emotional issues with a clear head. By alleviating painful symptoms, perhaps for the first time, medications create an atmosphere of trust binding therapist and patient together. They help solidify the alliance so that therapy can proceed.

COMBINATION TREATMENT

Why have medications been only partially helpful in treating the problem(s) of kleptomania? There are four reasons:

1) Kleptomania is a problem driven not exclusively by disrupted brain cells but is manufactured and packaged by people in distress.
2) As such, sufferers need human beings to help them sort through their distress.
3) Kleptomaniacs can't enter into an exclusive relationship with a pill.
4) Patients can't enter into a relationship with a pill and expect that it will solve all their problems.

Medications have actually revolutionized treatment in many areas. When used for the proper reasons, medication has been instrumental in treating patients suffering from kleptomania in slowing down the urge to steal, but has done so for different reasons. As we've seen, kleptomania appears to be more associated with character or personality issues than with simple depression. As any psychiatrist will attest, it's very difficult to treat or change personality.

When Lara, Paula, Susan, and the others first entered the world of treatment without the benefit of psychotherapy or any of the biological treatments, they were at times literally paralyzed by fear, anxiety and depression. Most of the time death was the only thing on their minds. Today, while Lara, Paula, and Susan still periodically steal (less so than ever), they're also doing something they've never really been able to do before—they're engaged in the long-term process of psychotherapy in order to help sort out and solve their emotional problems including kleptomania. Why? How? While their dedication to recovery is the primary reason they are progressing, without the newer biological therapies, including medications, it's unlikely they could have had enough clarity of thought to proceed.

Combination therapy, the treatment that couples one form of therapy with another, seems best equipped to help lessen the burden of theft. How do others feel about it? Even psychiatrists involved mainly in the art and science of psychotherapy agree. In his article entitled *Psychoanalytic Psychotherapy for a Woman with Diagnoses of Kleptomania and Bulimia*, and in discussing kleptomania, Schwartz maintains that "high doses of serotinergic (sic) antidepressants may reduce such impulses. Although the improvement may only be temporary, it allows time for the patient to verbalize and understand affects stimulated within the transference rather than merely acting on them."

What does this mean? It means that medications like Prozac, Paxil, Zoloft, and Luvox, as well as others, can be used in psychotherapy as a means of helping the patient talk about issues rather than acting them out. Does it cure stealing? Not likely. As we've seen, even my own patients feel better on medications and their depression seems to remit. However, because stealing is ingrained in their character structure and forms part of how they define themselves, they still steal. Combining different forms of treatment seems well advised.

Because it's specifically molded for a given patient and her issues, combination treatment probably offers the greatest chance of "success."

While most therapists are experienced mainly in psychotherapy and medication management, there are other forms of such combination therapies which may succeed in reducing or solving the problem of kleptomania. Combination treatment may also encompass psychotherapy, medications *and* behavioral modification. Let's take a look at a few specific cases where behavioral treatments were added. Fishbain used insight oriented and supportive therapies for the kleptomania patient's "risk-taking" behavior and guilt feelings. The therapist also ordered medication for the sufferer's depression and used behavioral modification for working on the actual theft. Interestingly, however, Fishbain noted that depression and stealing in his patient returned upon discontinuation of antidepressant medication. On the other hand, Gudjonsson successfully utilized a multi-disciplinary approach including relaxation training, family therapy and behavioral techniques to treat a woman with a twenty-year history of stealing.

SHOPPING AVOIDANCE

The least desirable form of "treatment" is the kleptomania sufferer's self-imposed ban on all shopping. This poor (but understandable) form of treatment probably constitutes the most common attempt by sufferers trying to help themselves. Unfortunately, this self-imposed treatment results in further isolation. It also means that the patient is probably not engaged in real treatment. While there have been several reports of this form of self-treatment, I'm certain it may be even more common than reported.

I've had numerous patients tell me that prior to treatment they've tried, often in vain, to remain at home, away from retail stores. Periodically they're successful. The realities of life, however, prevent this form of treatment from working with any great efficiency. The implications are important. When patients choose to cloister themselves, it means that they've reached a certain level of desperation that can really only be treated by a caring professional.

CHAPTER 19

Final Words About the Biology of the Human Condition

Although medications have really dominated the news, it should be remembered that unlike treatment for diabetes or high blood pressure, there aren't any standard, certain treatments for a troubled soul. That is, everyone's emotional blueprints are different: we have all been formed uniquely and over many generations. If we're unable to "standardize" a human being, it seems unlikely we'll be able to standardize biological treatment. The good news is that during the past ten years or so there has been an explosion in research and in the development of new, well-tolerated biological therapies that can greatly reduce the misery associated with kleptomania and its various "add-on" clinical problems. This should come as welcome relief to thousands.

RECOMMENDATIONS FOR KLEPTOMANIA SUFFERERS

As we've seen, the complexities of people—their attitudes, beliefs, personalities, personal histories, and biology—preclude easy answers to a very complicated set of emotional problems. The interplay among all these important human characteristics, including personality structure, emotional needs, and desires, makes kleptomania a formidable disorder in every way. It is not a disorder which can be self treated. Given this observation, how should treatment proceed?

Clearly, the initiation of therapy with a caring interested therapist or counselor is the first step. Such treatment must focus, first, on forming a solid therapeutic alliance with a psychotherapist. No alliance, no compliance—it's plain and simple. It's also important to work with a mental health professional who displays flexibility and who is ready and willing to refer the patient to another clinician, either a behavioral therapist or psychopharmacologist, should the need arise.

Will treatment be successful? Perhaps the most important issue to consider is whether or not the person suffering from kleptomania truly wants to give up stealing. Personal motivation plays an important part in willingness to change. In ridding oneself of kleptomania it plays a key part. When therapy is sought, it should provide the patient with a safe, comfortable forum, a place where he or she can weigh the risks and benefits of stealing cessation versus continuation. A suitable holding environment in which ambivalence can readily be tolerated by both patient and therapist is crucial as well. As we have seen, many people suffering from kleptomania have other serious problems such as suicidal ideation and disturbed interpersonal skills which can sometimes test a therapist and the therapeutic relationship. Susan, for example, frequently threatened suicide while in my office.

If the therapy is headed more towards stealing cessation strategies than dealing with other life issues as well, then it's a good idea for the patient to enter into an informal "contractual" agreement with the therapist to help determine the extent and pattern of the problem. This agreement involves a decision by the patient to make full disclosure of all stealing episodes. This involves charting and documentation about when the episodes took place, where they happened, what items were taken, and what, if anything, the patient was thinking or feeling at the time. Although this is really the only way to accurately track stealing and perhaps even obtain a glimpse into the person's mind during the episode, I find that such a "contract" is tough for the patient to agree to. Remember, no patient is likely to disclose this information until a firm alliance has been formed. This can sometimes become a lengthy process as it was in Susan's case. More times than not, the stealing episodes will seem quite patternless. However, if the patient is willing to keep a personal log or diary which tracks thoughts, feelings, and behaviors, this can be an invaluable aid to treatment.

If treatment does not seem to be working, what's next? If psychotherapy alone is not precipitating a decrease in stealing, consideration should be given to combination treatment. A referral to a behavioral specialist and/or psychopharmacologist for a trial of medication should be made. Since they are safe, well-tolerated by the body, and may be effective for the treatment of certain kinds of repetitive behaviors, SRI's are probably the best first choice if the medication route is chosen.

For sure, the mending of a kleptomania patient requires increased understanding, as well as commitment, strength, support, perseverance, and courage both on the part of the caregiver and patient.

LAST THOUGHTS

Throughout this book we've explored the lives of many different people. For those like Lara, Beth, Paula, and Susan, their treatment paths have been difficult ones with twists, turns, and disappointments complicating their already complicated lives. Despite the trials and tribulations, their worries, concerns and fears, as well as their repetitive thefts of unneeded objects, one thing is clear: their strength, dedication and perseverance in seeking cessation of their "impulse stealing" have seen them through the tough times.

While their struggles continue, all these women have been made better by their commitment to the healing process. Seeking out a ready ear, "confessing" their "sins," taking the time to sit, think, and talk, and working towards better lives for themselves and their families have brightened their previously dreary horizons. As hard as it is to believe, this amazing, adaptive mechanism—kleptomania, the tip of a complex iceberg of clinical issues—has been instrumental in their ongoing recoveries. Signaling far more depth to their emotional issues, the red flag of kleptomania unknowingly pushes them towards health and forces further psychological exploration.

I deem it a success when a patient makes the often very difficult but correct decision not to go through his or her pain alone. That's half the treatment. For the patient suffering from kleptomania, his or her personal battle has scored a victory when he or she decides to seek help.

While there is much we don't know, it is my hope that with personal courage, hope and a willingness to tolerate ambiguity and uncertainty, patient, therapist and researcher alike will reap the benefits of working together to solve the mysteries of kleptomania.

About the Author

Marcus Jacob Goldman, M.D. trained in general psychiatry at Harvard Medical School, where he also completed the Gaughan Fellowship in Forensic Psychiatry. Dr. Goldman is a member of the Program in Psychiatry and the Law at Harvard—a think tank that explores the legal aspects of mental health policies and practices. He has taught psychiatry and behavioral health at Harvard, has published numerous articles on a wide variety of mental health issues, and is the author of *The Joy of Fatherhood: The First Twelve Months*. Dr. Goldman is also the co-founder of "Board Exam Prep," an organization dedicated to helping psychiatrists successfully complete their board examinations. He is board certified in general, geriatric, and forensic psychiatry. He currently practices psychiatry, consults for New England Geriatrics and lives in Massachusetts.

Bibliography

Abelson, E. S. "The Invention Of Kleptomania." *Journal of Women in Culture and Society* (1989). 15:123-143.

Abraham, K. *Manifestations of the Female Castration Complex* in *Selected Papers on Psychoanalysis*. New York: Basic Books, 1953.

Abrahamsen, D. *Crime and the Human Mind*. New York: Columbia Press, 1964.

Aichorn, A. *Wayward Youth*. New York: Viking Press, 1935.

Alexander, F., and W. Healy. *Roots of Crime*. New York: Alfred A. Knopf, 1935.

Allen, A. "Stealing As Defense." *Psychoanalysis Quarterly* (1965). 34: 572.

Arbodela-Florez, J., H. Durie, and J. Costello. "Shoplifting—An Ordinary Crime?" *International Journal of Offender Therapy and Comparative Criminology* (1977). 21: 201-207.

Arieff, A. J., and C. G. Bowie. "Some Psychiatric Aspects Of Shoplifting." *Journal of Clinical Psychopathology* (1947). 8: 565-576.

Avery, N. C. "Family Secrets." *Psychoanalytic Review* (1982). 69: 471-486.

Baum, A., and E. M. Goldner. "The Relationship Between Stealing And Eating Disorders: A Review." *Harvard Review of Psychiatry* (1995). 3: 210-221.

Beldoch, M. "Stolen Objects As Transitional Objects." *American Journal of Psychiatry* (1991). 148: 1754.

Benedek, T. F. *Sexual Function in the Woman and Their Disturbances,* in *American Handbook of Psychiatry.* Edited by S. Arieti. New York: Basic Books, 1960.

Bergler, E. *The Basic Neurosis.* New York: Grune and Stratton, 1949.

Bleuler, E. *Textbook of Psychiatry.* New York: Macmillan Pub. Co., 1924.

Bradford, J., and R. Balmaceda. "Shoplifting: Is There A Specific Psychiatric Syndrome?" *Canadian Journal of Psychiatry* (1983). 28: 248-253.

Burstein, A. "Fluoxetine-Lithium Treatment For Kleptomania." *Journal of Clinical Psychiatry* (1992). 53: 28-29.

Casper, R. C., E. D. Eckert, K. A. Halmi, et al. "Bulimia." *Archives General Psychiatry* (1980). 37: 1030-1035.

Castelnuovo-Tedesco, P. "Stealing, Revenge And The Monte Cristo Complex." *International Journal of Psychoanalysis* (1974). 55: 169-177.

Castro, P. "Martha, My Dear." *People Magazine* (1991). September 23.

Chadwick, M. "A Case of Kleptomania In A Girl Of Ten Years." *International Journal of Psychoanalysis* (1925). 6: 300-312.

Chiswick, D. "Shoplifting, Depression And An Unusual Intracranial Lesion (A Case Report)." *Medical Science Law* (1976). 16: 266-268.

Church, R. "Dark Secret." *Nursing Times* (1988). 84: 42-43.

Coid, J. "Relief of Diazepam - Withdrawal Syndrome By Shoplifting." *British Journal of Psychiatry* (1984). 145: 552-554.

Cooper, A. M., A. Francis and M. Sacks. *The Psychoanalytic Model in Psychiatry.* Edited by R. Michels, A. M. Cooper, S. B. Guze, et al. New York: J. B. Lippencott , 1990.

Cupchik, W., and J. D. Atcheson. "Shoplifting: An Occasional Crime Of The Moral Majority." *Bulletin of the American Academy of Psychiatry Law* (1983). 11: 343-352.

Davis, H. "Psychiatric Aspects Of Shoplifting." *South African Medical Journal* (1979). 55: 885- 887.

Demitrack, M. A., F. W. Putnam, T. D. Brewerton, et al. "Relation Of Clinical Variable To Dissociative Phenomena In Eating Disorders." *American Journal of Psychiatry* (1990). 147: 1184-1187.

Elizur, A., and R. Jaffe. "Stealing As A Pathological Symptom." *Isr. Journal of Psychiatric Relat. Sci.* (1968). 6: 52-61.

Ellenberger, H. F. *The Discovery of the Unconscious*. New York: Basic Books, 1970.

Esquirol, E. *Treatise on Insanity*. Philadelphia: Lea and Blanchard. 1845.

Favazza, A. R. *Bodies Under Siege: Self-Mutilation in Culture and Psychiatry*. Baltimore: John Hopkins University Press, 1987.

——— , and R. J. Rosenthal. "Diagnostic Issues In Self-Mutilation." *Hospital and Community Psychiatry* (1993). 44: 134-139.

Fenichel, O. *The Psychoanalytic Theory of Neurosis*. New York: W. W. Norton and Co., Inc., 1945.

Fishbain, D. A. "Shoplifting As A Symptom of Stress in Families of Mentally Handicapped Persons: A Case Report (Letter)." *British Journal of Psychiatry* (1988). 153: 713.

——— "Kleptomania As Risk-Taking Behavior In Response To Depression." *American Journal of Psychotherapy* (1987). 41: 598-603.

Friedman, M. "Kleptomania: The Analytic And Forensic Aspects." *Psychoanalytic Review* (1930). 17: 452-470.

Gauthier, J., and D. Pellerin. "Management Of Compulsive Shoplifting Through Covert Sensitization." *Journal of Behavioral. Ther. Exp. Psychiatry* (1982). 13: 73-75.

Gibbens, T. C. N., and J. Prince. *Shoplifting.* London: ISTD, 1962.
———— "Shoplifting." *Med. Leg. Journal* (1962). 30: 6-19.
Glover, E. *Selected Papers on Psychoanalysis, Vol. 2.* New York:
    International Universities Press, Inc., 1960.
Glover, J. "A Case Of Kleptomania Treated By Covert Sensitization."
    British Journal of Clinical Psychology (1985). 24: 213-214.
Goldman, M. J. "Kleptomania: Making Sense Of The Nonsensical."
    American Journal of Psychiatry (1991). 148: 986-996.
———— "Kleptomania." *Directions in Psychiatry* (1992). 12: 3-7.
———— "Is There A Treatment For Kleptomania?" *Harvard Mental
    Health (Letter)* (1991). November issue.
———— "On Kleptomania" (Letter). *The American Journal of
    Psychiatry* (1992). 149: 848.
———— "Kleptomania: An Overview." *Psychiatric Annals* (1992).
    February issue.
———— "Letter To Editor." *Self* (1992). May/June issue.
———— "Kleptomania: Reply To Cupchik (Letter)." *American
    Journal of Psychiatry* (1991). August issue.
Gudjonsson, G. H. "The Significance Of Depression In The
    Mechanism Of Compulsive Shoplifting." *Med. Sci. Law.*
    (1987). 27: 171-176.
Guidry, L. S. "Use of A Covert Punishing Contingency In
    Compulsive Stealing." *Journal of Behavior Therapy and
    Exp. Psychiatry* (1975). 6:169.
Gutheil, T. G., and L. L. Havens. "The Therapeutic Alliance:
    Contemporary Meanings And Confusions." *Int. Rev.
    Psychoanalysis.* (1979). 6: 467-480.
Guze, S. B. *Criminality and Psychiatric Disorders.* New York:
    Oxford University Press, 1976.
Hatsukami, D., J. E. Mitchell, E. Eckert, et al. "Characteristics Of
    Patients With Bulimia Only, Bulimia With Affective
    Disorder, And Bulimia With Substance Abuse Problems."
    Addictive Behavior (1986). 11: 399-406.

Herderson, D., and I. Batchelor. *Textbook of Psychiatry*. London: Oxford Press, 1962.

Herman, J. L. *Father-Daughter Incest*. Cambridge, Massachusetts: Harvard University Press, 1981.

Hernandez, E. "Shoplifting: A Big-Ticket Item For Retailers." *Boston Globe* (1993). November 3 issue.

Hudson, J. I., H. G. Pope, J. M. Jonas, et al. "Phenomenologic Relationship Of Eating Disorders To Major Affective Disorders." *Psychiatry Res.* (1983). 9: 345-354.

Hunter, R., and I. Macalpine. *Three Hundred Years of Psychiatry*. London: Oxford University Press, 1963.

Jacobson, A. "Physical And Sexual Assault Histories Among Psychiatric Outpatients." *American Journal of Psychiatry* (1989). 146: 755-758.

James, I. P. "A Case Of Shoplifting In The Eighteenth Century." *Med. Sci. Law* (1977). 17: 200-202.

Jenike, M. A. "Trichotillomania" (Letter). *New England Journal of Medicine* (1990). 322: 472.

Keutzer, C. S. "Kleptomania: A Direct Approach To Treatment." *British Journal of Med. Psychol.* (1972). 45: 159-163.

Khan, K., I. C. A. Martin. "Kleptomania As A Presenting Feature Of Cortical Atrophy." *Acta Psychiatric Scand.* (1977). 56: 168-172.

Kligerman, C. "A Discussion Of The Paper By Pietro Castelnuovo-Tedesco On Stealing, Revenge And The Monte Cristo Complex." *Int. Journal of Psychoanalysis* (1974). 55: 179-181.

Krahn, D. D., K. Nairn, B. A. Gosnell, et al. "Stealing In Eating Disordered Patients." *Journal of Clinical Psychiatry*. (1991). 52: 112-115.

Laughlin, H. P. *The Neuroses in Clinical Practice*. Philadelphia: Saunders, 1956.

Levy, E. "Psychoanalytic Treatment Of A Child With A Stealing Compulsion." *American Journal of Orthopsychiatry* (1934). 4: 1-23.

Lister, E. D. "Forced Silence: A Neglected Dimension Of Trauma." *American Journal of Psychiatry* (1982). 139: 872-876.

McConaghy, N., and A. Blaszczynski. "Imaginal Desensitization: A Cost-Effective Treatment In Two Shoplifters And A Binge-Eater Resistant To Previous Therapy." *Australian/New Zealand Journal of Psychiatry* (1988). 22: 78-82.

McElroy, S. L., H. G. Pope, J. I. Hudson, et al. "Kleptomania: A Report Of 20 Cases." *American Journal of Psychiatry* (1991). 148: 652-657.

————, P. E. Keck, H. G. Pope, et al. "Pharmacological Treatment Of Kleptomania And Bulimia Nervosa." *Journal of Clinical Psychopharmacology* (1989). 9:358-360.

Meares, R. "The Secret." *Psychiatry* (1976). 39: 258-265.

Medlicott, R. W. "Fifty Thieves." *New Zealand Medical Journal* (1968). 67: 183-188.

Menaker, E. "A Contribution To The Study Of The Neurotic Stealing Symptom." *American Journal of Orthopsychiatry* (1939). 9: 368-378.

Mendez, M. F. "Pathological Stealing In Dementia." *Journal of the American Geriatric Society* (1988). 36: 825-826.

Meyers, T. J. "A Contribution To The Psychopathology Of Shoplifting." *Journal of Forensic Science* (1970). 15: 295-310.

Moak, G., B. Zimmer, and E. Stein. "Clinical Perspectives On Elderly First-Offender Shoplifters." *Hosp. Community Psychiatry* (1988). 39: 648-651.

Moore, R. "Shoplifting In Middle America: Patterns And Motivational Correlates." *International Journal of Offender Therapy and Comparative Criminology* (1984). 28: 53- 64.

Pierloot, R. A., W. Wellens, and M. E. Houben. "Elements Of Resistance To A Combined Medical And Psychotherapeutic Program In Anorexia Nervosa." *Psychoth. Psychosom.* (1975). 26: 101-117.

Pinel, P. *A Medico-Philosophical Treatise on Insanity.* Salem: Sheffield, Cadell and Davis, 1806.

Rado, S. "Fear And Castration In Women." *Psychoanalysis. Quarterly* (1993). 2: 459.

Ray, I. *A Treatise on the Medical Jurisprudence of Insanity.* Boston: Freeman and Bollen, 1838.

Roy, M. "Shoplifting As A Symptom Of Stress In Families Of Mentally Handicapped Persons: A Case Report." *British Journal of Psychiatry* (1988). 152: 845-846.

Russel, D. H. "Emotional Aspects Of Shoplifting." *Psychiatric Annals* (1973). 3: 77-86.

Schlueter, G. R., F. C. O'Neal, J. Hickey, et al. "Rational vs. Nonrational Shoplifting Types: The Implications For Loss Prevention Strategies." *International Journal of Offender Therapy and Comparative Criminology* (1989). 33: 227-239.

Schmideberg, M. "The Psycho-Analysis Of Asocial Children And Adolescents." *Int. Journal of Psychoanalysis* (1935). 16: 22-48.

Schwartz, H. J. "Psychoanalytic Psychotherapy For A Woman With Diagnosis Of Kleptomania And Bulimia." *Hospital and Community Psychiatry* (1992). 43: 109-110.

Segal, M. "Shoplifting" (Letter). *British Medical Journal* (1976). 1:960.

Simpson, C. A., and G. L. Porter. "Self-Mutilation In Children And Adolescents." *Bulletin of the Menninger Clinic* (1981). 45: 428-438.

Singer, B. A. "A Case Of Kleptomania." *Bulletin of the American Academy of Psychiatric Law* (1978). 66: 414-418.

Stone, M. H. *Individual Psychotherapy With Victims Of Incest In Treatment Of Victims Of Sexual Abuse.* Edited by R. P. Kluft. Philadelphia: W. B. Saunders Company, 1989.

Szasz, T. "Diagnoses Are Not Diseases." *Lancet* (1991). 338: 1574-1576.

"Teenage Bonnie and Klepto Clyde." Directed by John Sheppard, Produced and Written by Steve Jankowski, 1993.

Todd, J. "Pharmacogenic Shoplifting? (Letter)." *British Medical Journal* (1976). 1: 150.

Tolpin, P. H. "A Change In The Self: The Development And Transformation Of An Idealizing Transference." *International Journal of Psychoanalysis* (1983). 64: 461-483.

Turnbull, J. M. "Sexual Relationships Of Patients With Kleptomania." *Southern Medical Journal* (1987). 80: 995-997.

Van der Kolk, B. A. *The Compulsion To Repeat The Trauma, In Treatment Of Victims Of Sexual Abuse*. Edited by R. P. Kluft. Philadelphia: W. B. Saunders Company, 1989.

Volberg, R. A., and H. J. Steadman. "Refining Estimates Of Pathological Gambling." *American Journal of Psychiatry* (1988). 145: 502-505.

Whitaker, A., J. Johnson, D. Shaffer, et al. "Uncommon Troubles In Young People: Prevalence Estimates Of Selected Psychiatric Disorders In A Nonreferred Adolescent Population." *Archives of General Psychiatry*. 47:487-494.

Willensky, D. "Stolen Youth." *American Health* (1992). January/February issue: 40.

Winer, J. A., and G. H. Pollock. *Adjustment And Impulse Control Disorders, In Comprehensive Textbook Of Psychiatry*. Edited by H. I. Kaplan, A. M. Freedman, and B. J. Sadock. Baltimore: Williams and Wilkins, 1980.

Winnicott, D. W. *The Antisocial Tendency. Collected Papers*. London: Tavistock, 1958.

Wise, T. N. "Fetishism-Etiology And Treatment: A Review From Multiple Perspectives." *Comprehensive Psychiatry* (1985). 26: 249-257.

Wittels, F. "Some Remarks On Kleptomania." *Journal of Nervous Mental Disorders* (1929). 69: 241-251.

———— "Kleptomania And Other Psychopathic Crimes." *Journal of Criminal Psychopathology* (1942). 4: 205-216.

Wood, A., and M. E. Garralda. "Kleptomania In A 13-Year-Old Boy." *British Journal of Psychiatry* (1990). 157: 770-772.

Yagoda B. "Addicted To Stealing." *Self* (1994). February issue: 115-117, 154.

Yates, E. "The Influence Of Psycho-Social Factors On Non-Sensical Shoplifting." *International Journal of Offender Therapy and Comparative Criminology* (1986). 30: 203-211.

Zoric, F. J., P. J. Salis, T. Roth. Et al. "Narcolepsy And Automatic Behavior: A Case Report." *Journal of Clinical Psychiatry* (1979). 40: 194-197.

Appendix

KLEPTOMANIA & SHOPLIFTING
SELF-HELP RESOURCES

The individuals and organizations listed below do not necessarily sanction or approve any view, opinion, or treatment method described or endorsed in this book.

CALIFORNIA

• *Shoplifters Anonymous (SLA)*
PO Box 5463
Concord, CA 94524-5463
Contact: Dianna
East Bay area self-help group.

• *Anthropos Counseling Center*
326 South L Street
Livermore, CA 94550
Tel: (510) 449-7925
Contact: Jacqui Stratton, MFCC, Executive Director
Nonprofit counseling center providing ongoing counseling for those addicted to shoplifting/kleptomania.

CANADA

• **Dorothy & Leo Hickey**
180 Cherryhill Circle, Apt.601
London, Ontario
Canada N6H 2M2
Authors of *Shoplifting — A Cry for Help* (Dorle Publishing, 1996)

MICHIGAN

• **Cleptomaniacs & Shoplifters Anonymous (CASA)**
507 Lawrence
Ann Arbor, MI 48104
Tel: (313) 913-6990
E-mail: shulmann@umich.edu
Contact: Terrence D. Shulman, J.D., M.S.W., C.A.C.
Self-help organization founded in 1992. Two chapters of CASA meet in the Detroit area each week.

• **Lois Alexander, M.S.W., A.C.S.W.**
2041 Raybrook SE
Grand Rapids, MI 49503
Tel: (616) 942-1940
E-mail: lalex1@juno.com
Ms. Alexander provides individual and group psychotherapy specific to shoplifting.

• **Project Intervene**
Retail Fraud Group
61st District Court
333 Monroe NW
Grand Rapids, MI 49503
Tel: (616) 771-6490
Fax: (616) 771-6498
Group for court-ordered clients only.

• *Shoplifters against Temptation (SAT)*
2041 Raybrook SE
Grand Rapids, MI 49503
Tel: (616) 942-1940
Contact: Lois Alexander, M.S.W., A.C.S.W., Consulting Psychotherapist
Group meets Thursday evenings at 7:00 P.M. in Room 5118, Kent Community Hospital, 750 Fuller Avenue NE, Grand Rapids, MI.

MINNESOTA

• *Shoplifters Anonymous (SLA)*
PO Box 24515
Minneapolis, MN 55424
E-mail: mplssla@aol.com
Minneapolis are self-help group

NEW YORK

• *Shoplifters Anonymous*
c/o New York City Self Help Center
Tel:(212) 586-5770
New York City area self-help group.

NATIONAL

• *Shoplifters Alternative*
380 N. Broadway
Jericho, NY 11753-2109
Tel: (800) 848-9595
Fax: (516) 932-9393
Shoplifters Alternative is a national not-for-profit organization and division of Shoplifters Anonymous, Inc. The organization works with law enforcement and the courts to help people overcome a shoplifting problem by providing rehabilitation programs and ongoing support services.